THE MONGOLS AND GLOBAL HISTORY

A NORTON DOCUMENTS READER

NORTON DOCUMENTS READER SERIES

The Age of Jim Crow
Jane Dailey

The Global Revolutions of 1968
Jeremi Suri

Indian Removal
David S. Heidler and Jeanne T. Heidler

The Mongols and Global History
Morris Rossabi

1989: End of the Twentieth Century
James Carter and Cynthia Paces

Pirates in the Age of Sail
Robert Antony

Reforming America, 1815–1860
Joshua D. Rothman

Two Communities in the Civil War
Andrew J. Torget and Edward L. Ayers

THE MONGOLS AND GLOBAL HISTORY

A NORTON DOCUMENTS READER

Morris Rossabi
City University of New York

W. W. NORTON & COMPANY
New York / London

W. W. Norton & Company has been independent since its founding in 1923, when William Warder Norton and Mary D. Herter Norton first published lectures delivered at the People's Institute, the adult education division of New York City's Cooper Union. The firm soon expanded its program beyond the Institute, publishing books by celebrated academics from America and abroad. By mid-century, the two major pillars of Norton's publishing program—trade books and college text—were firmly established. In the 1950s, the Norton family transferred control of the company to its employees, and today—with a staff of four hundred and a comparable number of trade, college, and professional titles published each year—W. W. Norton & Company stands as the largest and oldest publishing house owned wholly by its employees.

Printed in the United States of America
First Edition

Composition by Westchester Book Group.
Manufacturing by Maple-Vail Book Manufacturing Group.
Production manager: Eric Pier-Hocking

Library of Congress Cataloging-in-Publication Data

The Mongols and global history : a Norton documents reader / [compiled by] Morris Rossabi. — 1st ed.
p. cm. — (Norton documents reader series)
Includes bibliographical references and index.

ISBN 978-0-393-92711-5 (pbk.)

1. Mongols—History—To 1500—Sources. I. Rossabi, Morris.

DS19.M647 2011
950'.2—dc22

2010036478

W. W. Norton & Company. Inc., 500 Fifth Avenue, New York, N.Y. 10110
www.wwnorton.com

W. W. Norton & Company Ltd., Castle House, 75/76 Wells Street, London W1T 3QT

1 2 3 4 5 6 7 8 9 0

CONTENTS

PREFACE

No other group or people were as renowned—or, to some of their enemies, as infamous—in the thirteenth- and fourteenth-century world as the Mongols. This casebook attests to their fame. The sources in this book are English translations of Armenian, Arabic, Chinese, Franco-Italian, Italian, Korean, Latin, Persian, Russian, Syriac, and Tibetan records. Writings in Georgian, Japanese, and Javanese could also have been chosen. Contemporaries from Venice to Kyoto wrote about the Mongols. It would be hard to find any group in history whose sudden appearance so many cultures and civilizations would notice. Judging from these travel accounts, histories, and personal reflections in this plethora of languages, the Mongol invasions and subsequent rule over the largest contiguous land empire in world history had a dramatic impact.

The foreign descriptions of the Mongol empire far outnumber the *Secret History of the Mongols*, the sole contemporary Mongolian source on this era. Discovered in the nineteenth century, it covers only early Mongol history through Chinggis Khan's death and his son's accession to power. Thus the image of the Mongols derives from the writings of their enemies, most of whom they subjugated. The reader must bear this in mind in evaluating such sources. Biases cannot but help to intrude in these writings.

The extraordinary geographic and linguistic range of the sources in this casebook testifies to the Mongols' role in world history. Their conquests brought Europe and East Asia in touch with one another, and their era could be described as the onset of global history. Civilizations throughout Eurasia would, for the first time, have political relations, which would lead to cultural, technological, artistic, commercial, and scientific exchanges. They often benefited from these exchanges, prompting Europeans to seek an easier and safer seaborne route to Asia. Such explorations, in turn, led to Vasco da Gama's voyage around the Cape of Good Hope to Asia and to Christopher Columbus's travels to the Americas. Thus, the study of global history begins with the Mongols.

This casebook can be used to supplement textbooks in courses on Asian history and world history. The primary sources are the central focus because exposure to the words and thoughts of contemporaries is the optimal way of attempting to understand them. Students and other readers who find the story of the Mongols compelling and want to learn more about them and this era in world history can turn for help to the "For Further Reading" section at the end of this volume. Limited space does not permit consideration of many aspects of the Mongol empire. Indeed, the Chaghadai Khanate of Central Asia, one of the four principal segments of the Mongol domains, gets short shrift, partly because it is the least studied of the Chinggisid lands. To be sure, the venue for several of the sources in the casebook is Central Asia, but those focus mostly on the Mongol invasions and on a dialogue with Chinggis Khan and do not reveal much about Mongol rule and influence on the region. The Chaghadai Khanate eventually gave rise to Tamerlane, the Central Asian ruler who carved out an enormous empire in Asia, a critical development in history. More research and English translations of other sources on the region may appear in the future and could be used to supplement this casebook.

I have devised questions about the implications and significance of these primary sources, but instructors and students may want to fashion their own questions based on their interests and views of the Mongols' impact on the thirteenth- and fourteenth-century world.

One technical note: I have retained umlauts but have omitted other diacritical marks because they can be distracting to the student and general reader and do not help in pronunciation of terms and names.

I am grateful to my wife, Mary, who has been with me on my Mongol travels and has carved out her own career in Mongol studies. It would be impossible to detail her manifold contributions to this casebook. Amy, Anna, Julia, and Tony Rossabi and Howard, Sarah, and Nathan Sterinbach also contributed to its completion. Over the years, I have learned much about the Mongol empire from conversations with colleagues, some of whom are gone but still vividly remembered. I want to thank, in particular, Joseph Fletcher Jr., Denis Sinor, Owen Lattimore, Pamela Crossley, David Morgan, William Honeychurch, Ladan Akbarnia, and Wu Pei-yi.

Part I
Introduction

> They came, they sapped, they burnt, they slew, they plundered and they departed.
> —Juvaini, *The History of the World Conqueror*

The image of Eastern invaders who blasted through Asia and Eastern Europe like a devastating hurricane, massacring hundreds of thousands of people and plundering the territories in their path, has been imprinted on the Western mind. The anonymity of "they" conveys the bewilderment of contemporaries from China to Hungary, who were suddenly confronted by a whirlwind of Mongol attacks. This perception of savagery and animal-like behavior was reinforced by the Mongols' lifestyle. Their dependence on animals for food, clothing, shelter, fuel, and medicines contributed to this image. Foreigners perceived their continual migrations to seek water and grass for their herds as evidence of their barbarism.

Yet their conquests, leading to the establishment of the largest contiguous land empire in world history, initiated the first contacts between Europe and East Asia and generated economic and cultural advances in the civilizations they ruled. The *Pax Mongolica* that they imposed on much of Asia, even though it was not free of all violence, facilitated travel and trade throughout their domains, leading to the first intimations of global history. Iranian miniature paintings, Chinese plays, and Russian gold vessels emerged from the ensuing cultural efflorescence.

How can these two disparate images of the Mongol empire be reconciled? Such attempts are hobbled because most of the primary sources were written by peoples the Mongols conquered. They would often portray their Mongol rulers in a negative light. Other than through the semimythical, semifactual *Secret History of the Mongols*, the Mongol side of the story cannot be presented. The Mongols developed a written language only early in the thirteenth century and scarcely had the time to evolve a tradition of historical writing. Despite these impediments, a careful and critical consideration of the East and West Asian and European sources can yield a somewhat more nuanced view of the Mongol influence on the world.

Origins

The Mongols relied on sheep, goats, and yaks or oxen for food, clothing, shelter, and transport, and their lives centered on seasonal moves to find water and grass for these animals. Bactrian camels enabled them to transport their household belongings on these journeys. Horses gave them a tactical advantage in conflicts with sedentary civilizations. Their ability to use the bow and arrow while riding gave them the upper hand in combat with foot soldiers.

However, a nomadic pastoral economy was precarious. The spread of disease among the livestock or a snowy winter or a summer drought could spell disaster. Most families had few reserves of food or other necessities because of their frequent migrations. The fragility of their economy prompted the Mongols to seek commerce with China and Central Asia, their neighbors. They obtained grain and craft articles and in return offered animals and animal products.

The religious practices of the early Mongols reflected their lifestyle. Because of their migrations, they could not build elaborate temples. They worshipped on hills or mountains where piles of stones (*ovoo*) had been carefully arranged. They prayed to mountains, stars, trees, fires, and rivers and, in particular, to Tenggeri ("Sky God"). By the twelfth century, shamans conducted ceremonies and acted as intermediaries between the dead ancestors and Tenggeri and the living.

The Mongol tribes were renowned for their martial skills, because all Mongol males received military training. However, in late-twelfth-century Mongolia, wars among the various tribes created havoc, and most hoped for a leader who could bring peace.

Chinggis Khan and Mongol Unity

Temüjin (1162?–1227) proved to be that leader. After his father was murdered when Temüjin was eight or nine years old, he learned how to survive in a daunting environment. His ability to forge blood brotherhoods (*anda*) with wealthier or more powerful leaders proved to be critical. The boost provided by this assistance from *andas* prompted him, sometime in the mid-1180s, to assume the title of "khan." However, around 1202, Temüjin and the Ong Khan, his principal *anda*, had become enemies. Temüjin gathered his troops and overwhelmed the Ong Khan's forces. This victory permitted him to attract more men to his side. In 1206, the chiefs of the leading tribes gathered together at an assembly (*khuriltai*) to endorse Temüjin as their ruler and to grant him the title of Chinggis Khan (or Genghis, as he is commonly known in the West), which meant "fierce ruler."

Numerous explanations have been offered for Chinggis's success in unifying the Mongols. His military prowess was significant, but his administrative and political skills were as crucial. One talent was his ability to forge alliances with influential leaders. Another was his policy of an equitable division of spoils. Still another lies in the organization he devised. He divided his people into chiliarchies, or groups of one thousand. This new organization was designed to undermine the authority of the old clan and tribal leaders, who would be superseded by commanders loyal to Chinggis.

Chinggis's Foreign Campaigns

How could Chinggis and his descendants, with command over fewer than a million people, have conquered such a vast domain? Part of the explanation lies in the state of decline in the regions they subdued. China, for example, was not united; in fact, foreign dynasties governed in the north. The Jurchen peoples of Manchuria had expelled the Song, the ruling dynasty of China, from the north in 1126, and the Song controlled only South China. The Khwarazmian Shah ruled Central Asia but faced considerable opposition. The rulers were Turks, but many of the inhabitants were Iranians. Even farther to the west, Russia had no central government that could resist the Mongol forces.

In 1207, Chinggis started his foreign campaigns by attacking the Tanguts, partly because their land in northwest China lay along the trade routes to Central Asia and Iran. In 1211, he initiated a campaign against the Jurchen Jin dynasty, and by 1215 his troops occupied Zhongdu (the area around modern Beijing). Then he turned his attention to Central Asia. A local governor had killed a large group of Mongol and Muslim merchants, accusing them, probably correctly, of espionage. The Shah had executed an envoy Chinggis had sent to demand that the governor be turned over for punishment. In 1219, Chinggis set forth with two hundred thousand troops for a campaign against the Shah. In 1220, Chinggis sacked the town of Bukhara, and his forces looted Samarkand and deported thirty thousand artisans eastward. The Iranian historians probably exaggerated the horrors of these campaigns, but no doubt the Mongols inflicted considerable damage on Central Asia.

On the way back toward northwest China for a second campaign against the Tanguts, Chinggis died in 1227. According to later accounts, his body was transported to the Burkhan Khaldun ("Buddha Cliff") in northeast Mongolia and was buried in a secret location there. However, some scholars argue that he was buried in the Ordos region of northwest China or closer to the location of his death.

Chinggis bequeathed a vast territory to his descendants, but his other legacies were even more important. One was his policy of religious toleration, which, he believed, would facilitate Mongol control over subjugated peoples. This toleration extended not only to different religions but also to different ethnic groups. Indeed, Chinggis relied on foreigners to assist him even before he became khan. In 1204, he commissioned a Turk to adapt a Turkic script to provide a written language for Mongol.

One of Chinggis's most significant legacies was the *Jasagh*, a set of rules and laws that concerned the military, governance, and justice and enforced Mongol taboos. Most of its regulations focused on nomadic pastoral society and could not be applied to a bureaucratic empire that ruled sedentary societies. The laws mandate punishments for horse thieves, describe the decimal system of organizing Mongols into groups of a thousand and ten thousand, and demand absolute obedience to the khan's dictates.

Chinggis's Successors

The lack of a precise and orderly means of succession proved to be part of the Mongols' undoing. A *khuriltai* composed of the leading Mongol nobles selected the Great Khan, who had to be one of Chinggis's direct descendants. Chinggis himself chose his son Ögödei in the only uncontested election to the Great Khanate.

Ögödei continued his father's military campaigns. In 1234, he defeated the Jin dynasty and occupied north China. In 1237, his nephew Batu crossed the Volga and, in quick succession, conquered Riazan, Moscow, Vladimir-Suzdal, and Kiev. He then launched a two-pronged assault on Eastern Europe. On April 9, 1241, his forces defeated Polish troops at Liegnitz. On April 11, Batu attacked Hungary and occupied Budapest. An attack on western Europe seemed inevitable. However, early in 1242, Batu withdrew and established his capital in Sarai on the lower Volga. One possible motive for Batu's precipitous withdrawal may have been the dearth of grasslands for the Mongol horses in western Europe. Another impetus was the death of Ögödei on December 11, 1241, which required Batu's attendance at a *khuriltai* to select a Great Khan.

Among Ögödei's other accomplishments was construction of a capital city in Khara Khorum in Mongolia, an indication that he intended to rule, not simply devastate the territories he had subjugated. However, Khara Khorum could not readily supply a growing population. Numerous carts and caravans arrived daily to provide food and other necessities for the population, a tremendous burden on the empire.

Changes in Succession

Ögödei's death created a power vacuum, because the Mongol nobility had not adopted an orderly system of succession. His youngest brother Tolui's sons were candidates for the Great Khanate. Tolui's wife, Sorghaghtani Beki, had groomed her sons to rule. Many contemporary writers considered her the most remarkable woman of her age. In her own North China lands, which Ögödei had granted as her domain, she promoted Chinese agriculture, recognizing that exploitation of the peasants was a short-sighted policy. Moreover, although she was an ardent Nestorian Christian, she supported Buddhism, Daoism, and Islam to win favor with her Chinese subjects.

However, she faced an indomitable foe, Ögödei's widow Töregene. The decade after Ögödei's death witnessed a conflict between two mothers to secure the Great Khanate for their sons, an indication of the power of elite Mongol women. Töregene initially had her son Güyüg enthroned as Great Khan in 1246, but he died in 1248, setting the stage for another struggle. After considerable violence, in 1251, the Mongol nobility enthroned Sorghaghtani Beki's son Möngke as the Great Khan. Ögödei's descendants insisted that Möngke's accession was illegitimate, leading to murders, bloody purges, and disunity. Ultimately, the territories subjugated by the Mongols fragmented into autonomous, occasionally warring states, eventually forming four distinct entities—East Asia, the Golden Horde in Russia, the Chaghadai Khanate in Central Asia, and the Il-Khanate in West Asia. Nonetheless, once Möngke ascended to the throne, he pursued the Mongols' expansionist policies. He assigned his brothers to the primary operations, Hülegü heading toward West Asia and Khubilai to campaign against the Song dynasty in China.

Khubilai: Great Khan and Emperor

Khubilai Khan now emerged on the historical stage. Having earlier received territories in North China, he devised a regular administrative system. With assistance from foreign advisers, he promoted agriculture, issued paper money, and collected taxes. His most important project was construction of a city in Shangdu, an indication that he had veered away from the Mongol nomadic lifestyle. Shangdu (known as "Xanadu" to Samuel Taylor Coleridge) resembled a typical Chinese city except for the hunting preserve, which reflected Khubilai's Mongol heritage.

In 1258, his brother Möngke commissioned him to lead an army to conquer the Southern Song dynasty. Möngke's troops headed south to capture the province of Sichuan and then march eastward. Khubilai's forces would cross the Yangzi river and engage the Song directly. Möngke made steady progress until his death in 1259. Khubilai and his brother Arigh Böke then struggled for the succession. Arigh Böke embodied the world of the steppes as the defender of the traditional Mongol ways, whereas Khubilai recognized the need for accommodations to the sedentary civilizations. After several significant defeats, in 1264, Arigh Böke surrendered.

As Great Khan, Khubilai sought to establish an administration that attracted Chinese support but also protected the Mongols. He refused, for example, to restore the Chinese civil service examinations because he wanted an international coterie of officials. Yet he retained the Chinese secretariat to help devise policy and six functional ministries to implement it.

Khubilai faced substantial economic and social problems. North China had not recovered from the Mongol conquests. Thus, in 1262, he founded the Office for the Stimulation of Agriculture. He also supported commerce by increasing the flow of paper currency, providing government loans for long-distance trade, and building roads and canals. Such governmental support resulted in increased trade across Asia and to cultural, religious, and artistic diffusion. Missionaries, singers, clerics, weavers, doctors, translators, silversmiths, astronomers, potters, and others traveled throughout the Mongol domains and introduced new ideas and techniques.

Khubilai needed to assert his legitimacy as a ruler of China. His transfer of the capital from Khara Khorum in Mongolia to Daidu (or Beijing) signaled an effort to ingratiate himself with the Chinese. He then sought to win over Confucians in his domain by choosing a Chinese name, Yuan or "origin," for his dynasty and by restoring the Confucian rituals of music and dance. Simultaneously, he recruited Muslims for government positions and permitted them considerable autonomy, with a Shaikh al-Islam, or elder, often serving as community leader. Such privileges encouraged Muslim merchants to trade with the rest of Asia and to assume positions as Yuan tax collectors and financial administrators.

Khubilai's appeals to the Buddhists had started even earlier. He quickly recognized that Tibetan Buddhism offered legitimacy because of its approval of political involvement. Khubilai was also impressed with the 'Phags-pa Lama, a Tibetan Buddhist who had joined his court. In 1261, he placed 'Phags-pa in charge of all Buddhist clergy, and 'Phags-pa then identified him with Manjusri, the Boddhisattva of Wisdom, and portrayed him as a *Chakravartin* or "Universal King," offering Khubilai greater legitimacy with Buddhists.

Khubilai's most important step in achieving legitimacy was conquest of the Southern Song dynasty. The eventual conflict centered on Xiangyang and Fancheng, two strongholds that protected the Middle Yangzi basin and the southeast coast. Khubilai needed a naval force and siege weapons to attack and overcome their resistance. As early as 1268, the Mongols laid siege to Xiangyang, and Khubilai recruited two West Asian Muslims to provide artillery support. The two men built mangonels and catapults that hurled huge rocks into the two cities. After five years of combat, Xiangyang surrendered in 1273. By 1276, the Mongols attacked the Song capital of Hangzhou, the world's most populous city. Acting in the name of her five-year-old grandson and emperor, the Empress Dowager surrendered the capital. Khubilai ensured that the Imperial family was well treated in order to ingratiate himself with the Chinese. Meanwhile loyalist officials fled from one port to another, with Mongol troops in hot pursuit. In 1279, surrounded by Mongol troops in China's southern extremity, the leading loyalist took the child emperor and jumped overboard to their death. The Song dynasty finally collapsed.

Khubilai and Culture

If Khubilai wished to gain in stature as ruler of China and as the Great Khan, he needed to be a patron of literature and the arts. Thus he assigned 'Phags-pa to create a written script for his domain's languages. The Tibetan cleric presented it in 1269, but his alphabet never replaced the Mongol script or the Chinese characters. Khubilai failed to recognize that government imposition of an artificially designed written language would not be readily accepted.

He and his fellow Mongols supported Chinese painters. Some painters, frustrated by "barbarian" rule, became recluses. However, just as many welcomed Mongol patronage, contributing to the efflorescence of Chinese painting. Khubilai supported Zhao Mengfu, the greatest Yuan painter. Later the Wenzong emperor founded the Pavilion of the Star of Literature where connoisseurs met to appreciate calligraphy and painting. Later still, Khubilai's great granddaughter added considerably to the Imperial Palace collections.

Crafts, especially porcelains and textiles, prospered because of Khubilai's favorable attitude toward beautiful objects. Chinese porcelains attracted him, partly because he recognized their value in trade throughout Asia. The Mongols also contributed to the renaissance of Chinese textiles. Their fondness for "cloths of gold" (*nasij*) inspired Chinese to produce clothing, banners, and Buddhist mandalas, with the use of gold thread.

Khubilai's construction projects necessitated the recruitment of foreign craftsmen, probably the most famous of whom was Aniko, a Nepalese architect and painter. The Court commissioned the young Nepalese to construct two Buddhist temples, a White Stupa in Daidu, a Daoist temple, statues of Confucius, and an armillary sphere and other astronomical instruments.

Khubilai in Decline

The year 1279 proved a watershed in Khubilai's reign. Until that time, he had scarcely failed in his undertakings, but appearances were deceptive. He needed considerable revenues to defray the expenditures on construction of Daidu and the resulting enlargement of the Grand Canal to supply its inhabitants, among other building projects. Ahmad, his Central Asian finance minister, enrolled additional households on tax lists, levied higher taxes on merchants, and earned additional income from government monopolies on salt, iron, tea, liquor, and gold and silver. These policies created numerous enemies, and in 1282, officials assassinated him and then persuaded Khubilai of Ahmad's corruption and treachery. Yet Ahmad's murder did not resolve the Mongols' financial problems. Throughout the 1280s, their revenue shortfalls became even more pressing.

Simultaneously, Khubilai's expeditions against Japan failed. The Japanese Shogun had repeatedly spurned the Mongols' orders of submission, leading to an abortive Mongol invasion in 1274. The Mongols made elaborate preparations for their next campaign. In June of 1281, a force from North China set forth for Kyushu, to be followed by a detachment from South China. On August 15, a typhoon struck the coast of Kyushu. Many Mongol ships sank, and the troops who had landed on Kyushu were stranded and quickly hunted down. The Japanese considered the typhoon to have been a "Divine Wind" or "Kamikaze."

Similarly, the Mongols' campaigns in Southeast Asia were ill-conceived. Seeking an expansion of their empire, the Mongols erred in not considering terrain and environment. Because horses were unsuited to forested lands, their cavalry was rendered ineffective. Guerilla warfare, heat, and disease took their toll on the Mongol armies. An attack on Annam (modern Vietnam) harmed both sides, leading the Annamese king to send an envoy reputedly to pledge loyalty in return for a cessation of hostilities. Even more disastrous was a naval expedition against Java in 1292. Guerilla attacks, the duplicity of Javanese allies, and the tropical heat forced the Mongol troops to retreat to their ships and to return to China.

These years also witnessed personal losses for Khubilai. His favorite and most influential wife, Chabi, died in 1281, and Crown Prince Jingim predeceased his father in 1285. These sorrows and his failed policies weighed heavily on Khubilai. He became grotesquely corpulent, contributing to serious health problems. Old age, weariness, disappointments, and excessive drinking and eating finally took their toll. He weakened, and on February 18, 1294, he died in his palace.

End of Mongol Rule in China

The Yuan's remaining seventy years witnessed its unraveling, severely curtailing China's contacts with the outside world. Instability inevitably translated into a lack of the diplomatic relations and the cultural, technological, and religious diffusion of the earlier Mongol era. Succession to the throne, the Mongols' perennial Achilles' heel, contributed once again to instability. Candidates had to be Khubilai's descendants, but this regulation offered considerable latitude. Conflicts often revolved around disputes between steppe Mongols and their cousins in the sedentary world who had accommodated to Chinese civilization. Violence erupted in 1307 before an emperor was enthroned; in 1323, a cabal assassinated the ruling emperor; in 1329, a half-brother killed the emperor and assumed the throne. The stability associated with Khubilai's long thirty-four year reign contrasted sharply with those of all but one of the emperors who succeeded him.

The courts' financial policies also created difficulties. The emperors provided grants to imperial princes and officials, a considerable burden on the Treasury. Corruption further bedeviled the courts and the emperors. Several emperors sought to reduce court expenditures and to increase revenues, through taxes on liquor, higher prices for salt licenses, and other fees, but these efforts failed. Court decadence was not checked, and revenue shortfalls prevented it from properly maintaining public works projects. This lack of attention contributed to a higher incidence of floods and droughts and ensuing famines than in earlier times. Plague and other diseases further undermined the Yuan.

The solutions proposed by some officials did not help. Toghto, a prominent reformer, tried to root out army corruption, impose control over rapacious authorities, and increase tax revenues. However, the last Yuan emperor, who had abandoned himself to religion and hedonism, resented Toghto and dismissed him.

Such problems notwithstanding, sinicized Mongol emperors devised policies that fostered cultural developments. In 1315, the Renzong emperor restored the traditional civil service examinations, ingratiating himself with Confucians. The same emperor patronized Chinese painters, and Guan Daosheng, the wife of the greatest Yuan painter, Zhao Mengfu, benefited from such support.

Nonetheless, disarray provoked by factional strife, official graft, and financial failures led to increased pauperization of the population and then banditry and eventually rebellion. Zhu Yuanzhang, one rebel leader, overwhelmed the others, and in 1368, his forces compelled the last Yuan emperor to flee to his ancestral homeland.

The cosmopolitanism of Khubilai's reign withered away, and the Mongols' vital links and contributions to global history ended.

Il-Khanate and West Asia

In 1253 Möngke had assigned his brother Hülegü to attack West Asia. Hülegü initially defeated the Ismailis (the Order of the Assassins). Then in 1258, his troops sacked Baghdad and destroyed the Abbasid Caliphate. Advancing to Syria, he challenged the Mamluks, the most significant Muslim dynasty in the Middle East. However, he learned of his brother Möngke Khan's death in 1259. Leaving a relatively small force behind, he headed back to participate in the election of the Great Khan. In 1260, a Mamluk army, capitalizing on Hülegü's departure, routed the token Mongol detachment in Ayn Jalut, ending the Mongol campaigns in West Asia.

Hülegü then proclaimed himself to be Il-Khan (or "Subordinate Khan") and established the Il-Khanate in Tabriz as a semi-autonomous Mongol domain. The Il-Khanate clashed with Russia's Mongol rulers, known as the Golden Horde, who claimed that Chinggis had granted the Western regions of the Empire to them. By 1262, the Il-Khanate's and the Golden Horde's troops battled along their borders, undermining Mongol unity. At the same time, Il-Khanate troops often fought with the Mongols of the Chaghadai Khanate in Central Asia.

Abakha, Hülegü's son, succeeded to his father's throne and employed a multi-religious and multi-ethnic officialdom to rule a largely Muslim population. However, Tegüder, Abakha's brother and successor, converted to Islam, leading to rebellion. Arghun, Abakha's son, defeated and executed Tegüder. More assassinations and rebellions plagued the Il-Khanate until the accession of Ghazan, Arghun's son. Simultaneously, in the almost eighty years of Il-Khanate rule, all but one of the viziers, or chief ministers, was executed or assassinated, the most telling indication of political instability.

Faced with internal disarray and foreign threats, the Il-Khans searched for allies among the Europeans, who sought a Crusade to oust the Mamluks from the Holy Lands. In 1287, Arghun dispatched Rabban Sauma, a Nestorian Christian, to propose a military alliance with the Europeans against the Mamluks. Rabban Sauma met with the Byzantine emperor, the kings of England and France, and the Pope and believed that he had forged an alliance. However, these potential allies were diverted by domestic insurrections, intra-European wars, and suspicions of Mongol intentions, and the only tangible evidence of Rabban Sauma's mission was his report, one of the first Eastern accounts of the West.

Unlike their armed struggles with the Mongol rulers of Russia and of Central Asia, the Il-Khans maintained good relations with the Yuan dynasty of China. They traded with each other, and the ensuing cultural diffusion was striking. Chinese doctors traveled to Central Asia and Iran; and Chinese plants enriched West Asian agriculture. Yuan court officials consulted Muslim and Nestorian Christian doctors, and Khubilai established an Institute of Muslim Astronomy. However, the impact of such cultural diffusion ought not to be overstated. Chinese astronomy and medicine remained Chinese, and Iranian agriculture and medicine continued to reflect Iranian traditions.

Chinese and Iranian art revealed the most tangible influence of Mongol rule. Mongol officials were superintendents of the blue-and-white porcelain production center, which produced wares for West Asian consumers. Mongol Khans compelled Central Asian weavers to move to China to create "cloth of gold" textiles. In turn, the Mongols' transmission of Chinese textiles and paintings prompted West Asians to employ Chinese motifs and to imitate scenes from Chinese landscape painting.

The accession of Ghazan as Il-Khan in 1295 introduced changes that affected such cultural interactions. Converting to Islam, Ghazan retained his identity as a Mongol, but he adopted the title of "Sultan." He destroyed Nestorian churches and Buddhist monasteries and dismissed non-Muslim bureaucrats. Differing from traditional Mongols who favored nomadic pastoralism, he supported peasants and promoted trade. Even more telling, he deviated from the Mongol practice of secret burials for rulers. Instead he constructed an Islamic-style mausoleum.

Ghazan's early death in 1304 curtailed the Il-Khanate's global interconnections and led to its final collapse. His brother Öljeitü built an imposing new capital in Sultaniyya and patronized the arts, but political problems persisted. Infighting resurfaced when he died prematurely, leaving his young son Abu Said as Il-Khan. The greatest tragedy of these chaotic conditions was the execution of the historian and vizier Rashid al-Din on false charges that he had poisoned the Il-Khan Öljeitü.

Internecine struggles, unscrupulous ministers, and increased taxes damaged Abu Said's reign. His early death in 1335 and his inability to produce a male heir doomed the dynasty. Il-Khanate rule collapsed, and regional leaders assumed power until the appearance of the conqueror Tamerlane in the late fourteenth century. Such unrest subverted relations with the Yuan dynasty and thus limited inter-civilization contact.

Despite political and economic instability, the Il-Khanate witnessed an Iranian renaissance, and Rashid al-Din exemplifies this cultural efflorescence. Trained as a physician, he was recruited into government and eventually became the vizier. His greatest achievement was the first world history, the *Compendium of Chronicles*. The Il-Khan Ghazan, concerned about the blurring of Mongol identity in Iran, commissioned him to write a history of the Mongols. Rashid al-Din transformed this assignment into a world history. Commissioned illustrations of the manuscript complemented and enriched his text.

Golden Horde

Because Mongol rule in Russia has received little attention, both myths and unproven assertions characterize depictions of this almost 270-year period. The latest study argues that Russians wanted the Mongol era to be portrayed as destructive and almost entirely negative. The relatively small number of Mongols who participated in the Russian campaigns contributed to the difficulties in gauging their impact. The commanders were generally Mongols, but many of the troops were Turkic peoples from Central Asia. Moreover, many of the Mongols remained in the steppelands while only a few gravitated to the cities.

The original Mongol campaigns led to much loss of life and destruction of property. Batu, Chinggis Khan's grandson, was the overall commander, and much of his success was based on disunity in Russia. He founded a capital city in Sarai, not far from the Volga River. By doing so, he signaled his intent to occupy these domains, which included the upper Volga lands, the territories up to the Ural Mountains, and the northern Caucasus, among other areas. Shortly thereafter, he confirmed his plans by dispatching agents (*basqaq*) who settled in these communities, conducted censuses, and collected taxes.

However, the accession of his brother Berke (r. 1257–1267) altered the earlier stability. Berke converted to Islam, which led to conflict with Hülegü, who established the Il-Khanate. Both also claimed Azerbaijan, and thus Berke often collaborated with his enemy's enemy, the Muslim Mamluks, in wars with the Il-Khans.

The Mongol Khans' policies in administering their newly subjugated domains (known later as the Golden Horde) resembled those of the other Mongol-ruled territories. They supported commerce, which offered them silk, porcelain, and glass among other goods, and provided markets for their craft articles, including gold objects. Like Mongol rulers elsewhere, they encouraged artisans or recruited them as forced laborers. They also tolerated foreign religions, including the Russian Orthodox Church.

Native princes who sought independence arose in the fourteenth century. Assuming some of the tax and other government responsibilities, Russian princes became more autonomous. The Muscovite princes, in particular, began to challenge Mongol rule. At a battle in 1380, Prince Dmitrii Ivanovich "Donskoi" defeated Mongol forces. Two years later, the Golden Horde, under the leadership of Tokhtamish with the assistance of the conqueror Tamerlane, recovered and defeated the Muscovites. However, by 1387, Tamerlane and Tokhtamish were at war, and in 1395 the Central Asian ruler crushed his previous ally. Tokhtamish lost his throne, and the Golden Horde fell into disarray. In 1502, Mengli Girai of the Crimea dealt the death blow to the Golden Horde.

What then was the Mongol influence on Russia? Until recent times, most Russian historians focused on the initial violence. On the other hand, Mongol weapons, strategy, and tactics provided models for the Russian State, which emerged in the sixteenth century. Mongol support for commerce led to Russia's participation in extensive trade networks. Mongol grants of land and tax-exempt status benefited the Orthodox Church, although its leaders remained hostile to the foreign rulers. In short, the Golden Horde fostered commercial and artistic interchanges.

The Mongols and the West

Rumors about the Mongols had reached Europe as early as the 1220s, but the pace of such reports accelerated by the late 1230s. Mongol advances in Russia and Eastern Europe from 1237 to 1241 inspired fears about a possible invasion of Western Europe. Such concerns provoked Pope Innocent IV to dispatch an embassy to the Mongols. The Franciscan John of Plano Carpini carried two papal letters that demanded that the Mongols cease to assault Christian lands and to accept baptism and conversion to Christianity. His mission appeared to be a failure because the Mongols did not submit or change their policies. However, he returned with a valuable report, consisting partly of intelligence information and partly of a portrait of Mongol society.

A second embassy, led by the Franciscan William of Rubruck, reached the Mongols' homeland in Northeast Asia. The account he brought back to Europe offers a treasure trove of information about Mongol food, religions, clothing, the roles of women, and the production of *airagh*, the liquor made of fermented mare's milk.

The Il-Khanate's occupation of West Asia brought the Mongols in even closer touch with Europe. Seeking European assistance against the Mamluks, the Il-Khans sent several embassies to the West. These missions failed, but Venetian and Genoese merchants traded with the Mongols. Francesco Balducci Pegolotti, a fourteenth-century merchant who actually never traveled to Asia, wrote a detailed itinerary of the journey from Europe to China, describing the routes, the expertise required, and the distances between towns and oases. Trade with China persisted through the middle of the fourteenth century when the collapse of the Il-Khanate and the instability of the Yuan dynasty subverted this commerce.

Marco Polo (1254–1324) was the most famous traveler of mercantile background to travel to China. Marco's account of his travels and his sixteen-year stay in China, which a storyteller named Rusticello actually wrote, is one of the most renowned books in world literature and reflects the Mongol era's globalization. His description of Shangdu, Khubilai's summer palace, stimulated Samuel Taylor Coleridge to write "Kubla Khan," one of the most famous English-language poems. Marco's reports about Daidu, paper money, the postal station system, and the means of selecting concubines eventually made a great impression on Europeans. Although his account omitted such significant features of Chinese civilization as the writing system, chopsticks, and bound feet, recent discoveries in Chinese and Iranian texts attest that he reached China. Many Europeans initially greeted Marco's account with skepticism; yet it, in part, spurred European explorers, including Christopher Columbus, to seek a sea route to East and South Asia.

The interchanges between the Mongol world and Europe were not entirely positive. Aside from the massacres and destruction wrought by the Eastern invaders, the Mongols have been accused of inadvertently transmitting the plague along the Silk Roads, culminating in the onset of the Black Death. It is seductive to believe that trade and closer connections among civilizations facilitated the spread of diseases, including the plague. However, much more evidence will be required to confirm the relationship of the Mongols to the Black Death.

Mongol Legacy

The Mongols set the stage for Eurasian history by facilitating and then promoting commercial, political, and artistic relations among Chinese, Islamic, Russian, and European civilizations. More merchants, missionaries, and craftsmen traveled across the continents than in any other previous period. The thirteenth century witnessed the first direct and personal contact between Europe and China. Many Europeans traveled to the Mongol-ruled Yuan dynasty in China, while Rabban Sauma, a man born in China, arrived in Europe. Commerce and contact translated into considerable cultural, artistic, and technological, not to mention culinary and linguistic, diffusion, and the pace of such interchanges accelerated. Part of the Mongol cultural legacy was the construction of splendid capital cities in Shangdu, Daidu, Tabriz, and Sarai.

Mongol social attitudes were also remarkable. Their policy of religious toleration or at least lack of persecution was a step ahead of much of Eurasia. Such toleration, in part, permitted them to recruit skilled foreigners to assist them, a significant innovation. Even more surprising, Mongol elite women had considerable authority and power, including ownership of property. Not surprisingly, many Western commanders would study Mongol military tactics and strategy.

The Mongols did not transform, though they influenced, the major civilizations they subjugated. China reemerged as a Confucian society, but Tibetan Buddhism, to which it had been exposed by the Mongols, attracted several Ming (1368–1644) and Qing (1644–1911) dynasty emperors and some of their people. Despite the initial favor shown to Nestorianism and Buddhism in the Il-Khanate, Iran's populace never deviated from Islam, although Sufism came to the fore. Like most religions in the Mongol domains, Russian Orthodoxy certainly benefited from state support and exemptions, but it was an indigenous religion, which the Mongols did not influence.

The Mongol era had both positive and negative economic and political impacts on civilization. The increase in commerce during the Mongol era benefited merchants, oasis dwellers, and consumers. Agriculture retained its dominant position, but the Middle Eastern and, especially, European demand for Asian products they received during the *Pax Mongolica* prompted the age of exploration, an effort to discover a less hazardous and more efficient means of transport to Asia. The Mongols' political influence, although occasionally negative, was also significant. The native Ming dynasty, which expelled the Yuan, continued unjustifiably to fear a Mongol invasion of China. The Mongols never unified under a single leader, but Ming concerns about a Mongol threat resulted in greater consolidation of power in the emperors' hands and more despotic rule. Their political impact on Russia is controversial. Several historians have attributed the rise of Russian autocracy to adoption of the Mongols' governmental system. Yet others argue that the tsarist structure developed considerably after the waning and withdrawal of the Mongols, challenging the view of any direct connection. After the Il-Khanate collapsed, Iran fragmented into regional governments until Tamerlane conquered and reunited it in the late fourteenth century.

In short, the Mongols' most enduring legacy was to facilitate travel, trade, and direct contacts between Europe and South and East Asia, promoting both a commercial revolution and an age of exploration in the West. Their vision of a Mongol-ruled world faded, partly because they themselves splintered into at least four regions often at war with and thus weakening each other. However, they contributed enormously to globalization and global history.

Expansion of the Mongol Empire, 1219–1280

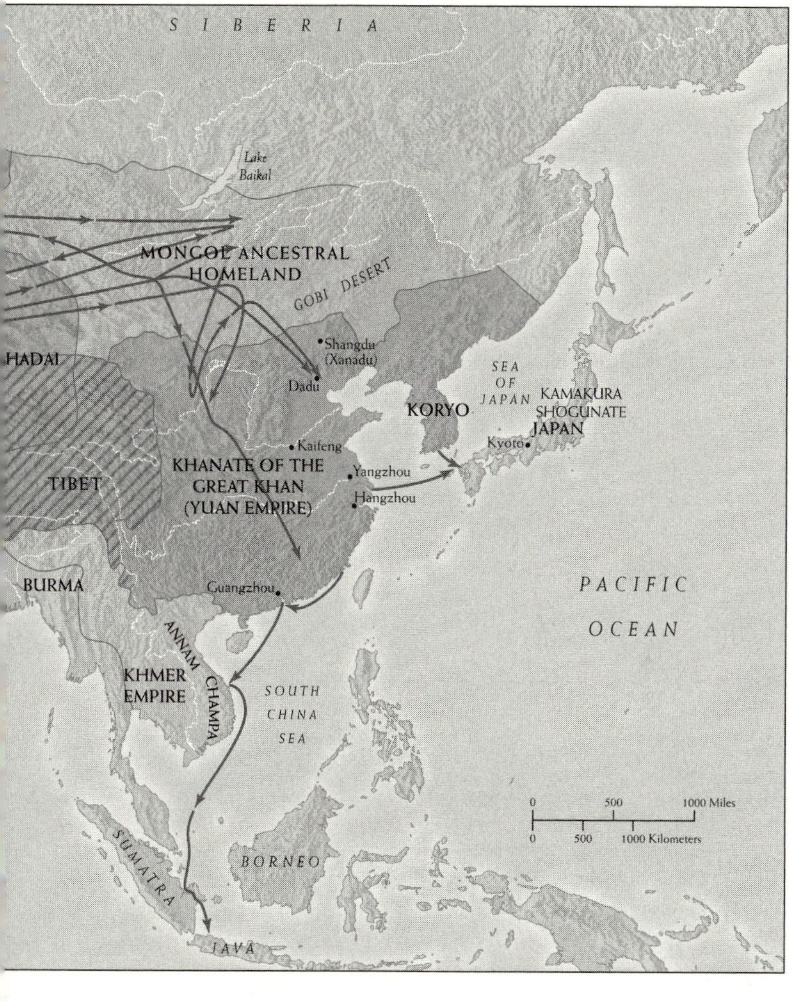

SIBERIA
Lake Baikal
MONGOL ANCESTRAL HOMELAND
GOBI DESERT
HADAI
Shangdu (Xanadu)
Dadu
SEA OF JAPAN
KAMAKURA SHOGUNATE JAPAN
KORYO
Kyoto
Kaifeng
KHANATE OF THE GREAT KHAN (YUAN EMPIRE)
Yangzhou
Hangzhou
TIBET
BURMA
Guangzhou
PACIFIC OCEAN
ANNAM
KHMER EMPIRE
CHAMPA
SOUTH CHINA SEA
0 500 1000 Miles
0 500 1000 Kilometers
SUMATRA
BORNEO
JAVA

Genealogical Charts of the Four Major Khanates

Great Khanate

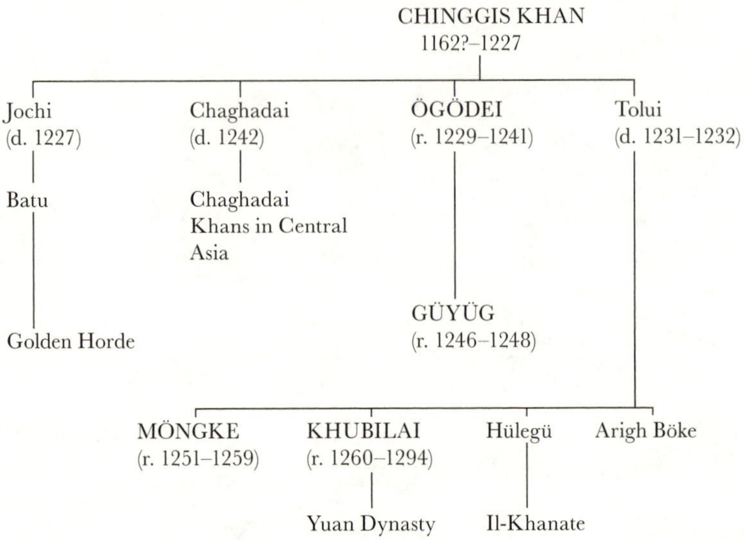

Il-Khanate

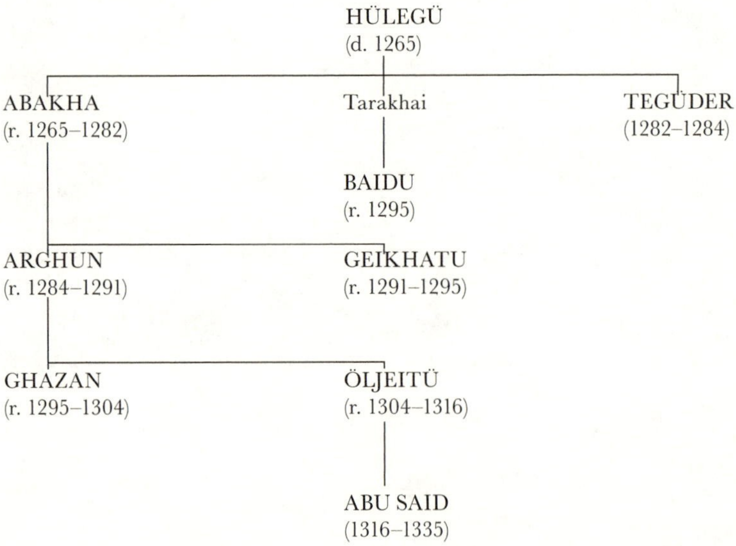

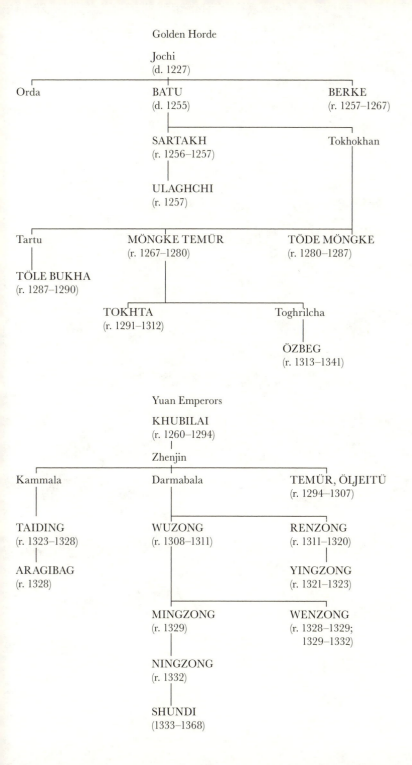

Golden Horde

Jochi
(d. 1227)

Orda

BATU
(d. 1255)

BERKE
(r. 1257–1267)

SARTAKH
(r. 1256–1257)

Tokhokhan

ULAGHCHI
(r. 1257)

Tartu

MÖNGKE TEMÜR
(r. 1267–1280)

TÖDE MÖNGKE
(r. 1280–1287)

TÖLE BUKHA
(r. 1287–1290)

TOKHTA
(r. 1291–1312)

Toghrilcha

ÖZBEG
(r. 1313–1341)

Yuan Emperors

KHUBILAI
(r. 1260–1294)

Zhenjin

Kammala

Darmabala

TEMÜR, ÖLJEITÜ
(r. 1294–1307)

TAIDING
(r. 1323–1328)

WUZONG
(r. 1308–1311)

RENZONG
(r. 1311–1320)

ARAGIBAG
(r. 1328)

YINGZONG
(r. 1321–1323)

MINGZONG
(r. 1329)

WENZONG
(r. 1328–1329;
1329–1332)

NINGZONG
(r. 1332)

SHUNDI
(1333–1368)

Part II
Mongol Lifestyle

Grigor of Akanc, History of the Nation of the Archers

Grigor of Akanc (ca. 1280–ca. 1335) was a monk at the Akner monastery who wrote an account of the Mongols, whom he referred to as "the Nation of the Archers." He was not as well educated as contemporary Armenian historians such as Kirakos of Ganjak, nor did he intend to write a history of Armenia. Because his history of the Mongols spanned the period from about 1230 to about 1270, most of his narrative dealt with events he could not have observed. The resulting work was thus not totally accurate and did not, on occasion, distinguish between fact and myth.

Now, however, we shall also tell what these first Tat'ars resembled for the first who came to the upper country were not like men. They were terrible to look at and indescribable, with large heads like a buffalo's, narrow eyes like a fledgling's, a snub nose like a cat's, projecting snouts like a dog's, narrow loins like an ant's, short legs like a hog's, and by nature *with* no beards at all. With a lion's strength they *have* voices more shrill than an eagle. They appear where least expected. Their women wear beautiful hats covered at the top with a head shawl of brocade. Their broad faces were plastered with a poisonous mixture of gum. They give birth to children like snakes and eat like wolves. Death does not appear among them, for they survive for three hundred years. They do not eat bread at all. Such were the first people who came to the upper countries.

Grigor of Akanc, "History of the Nation of the Archers," translated by Robert Blake and Richard Frye, *Harvard Journal of Asiatic Studies* 13.3–4 (1949): 295, 297.

DISCUSSION QUESTION

1. How does this selection play into Western stereotypes of the Mongols?

John of Plano Carpini, Mission to Asia

Pope Innocent IV dispatched John of Plano Carpini (d. 1252), a Franciscan missionary, as an emissary to the Mongols. Fearing that the Mongols would renew their military campaigns after their initial withdrawal from Hungary in 1241, the Pope sent John, a man probably in his sixties, to avert such a possibility. However, he undermined John's mission by having him transmit two papal bulls to the Mongol Khan. The bulls first proclaimed the Pope to be God's vicar and requested safe passage for John but then requested that the khan cease his campaigns, which "are laying [countries] waste in a horrible desolation" and "breaking the bonds of mutual ties, sparing neither sex nor age, you rage against all indiscriminately." The Mongol rulers, who perceived themselves to be superior to all others, would surely find these bulls objectionable.

Starting in 1246, John traveled across Central Asia, met Batu Khan of the Golden Horde, and witnessed the enthronement of Güyüg as Great Khan. The elaborate ceremonies and the valuable gifts sent by foreign states to the Great Khan impressed John and inspired even greater concern about the Mongol threat. Thus when Güyüg suggested that he wished to send ambassadors to accompany the papal envoy back to Europe, John, fearing that the Mongol emissaries would be spies or would notice European disunity or would be harmed and thus offer a pretext for an invasion, dissuaded the khan. He could not prevent Güyüg from sending a letter to the Pope demanding that Europe voluntarily submit to the Mongols or suffer the consequences. John returned to Europe with this inflammatory letter (see p. 120 for a translation of the letter), which was preserved in the Vatican Archives. Shortly thereafter, he became embroiled in an ecclesiastical court case and died in 1252 while it was being litigated.

John's mission would ordinarily be considered a failure, but the report he presented to the Pope proved invaluable. It described Mongol customs, beliefs, practices, and taboos and provided a brief history of Chinggis Khan and the Mongol conquests. As important, it offered analyses of their military tactics, their intelligence-gathering system, their sieges of important cities, and their use of cavalry. John himself warned Europe that the Mongols "never make peace except with those who submit to them" and that they intended "to bring the whole world into subjugation if they can."

Each man has as many wives as he can keep, one a hundred, another fifty, another ten—one more, another less. It is the general custom for them to marry any of their relations, with the exception of their mother, daughter and sister by the same mother. They can however take in marriage their sisters who have only the same father, and even their father's wives after his death; also a younger brother may marry his brother's wife after his death; or another younger relation is expected to take her. All other women they take as wives without any distinction and they buy them at a very high price from their parents. After the death of their husbands the women do not easily enter into a second union, unless a man wishes to take his stepmother to wife.

The clothes of both the men and the women are made in the same style. They do not use capes, cloaks or hoods, but wear tunics of buckram, velvet or brocade made in the following fashion: they are open from top to bottom and are folded over the breast; they are fastened on the left with one tie, on the right with three, on the left side also they are open as far as the waist. Garments of all kinds of fur are made in the same style; the upper one however has the hairy part outside and is open at the back; it also has a tail at the back reaching to the knees.

The married women have a very full tunic, open to the ground in front. On their head they have a round thing made of twigs or bark, which is an ell in height and ends on top in a square; it gradually increases in circumference from the bottom to the top, and on the top there is a long and slender cane of gold or silver or wood, or even a feather, and it is sewn on to a cap which reaches to the shoulders. The cap as well as this object is covered with buckram, velvet or brocade, and without this headgear they never go into the presence of men and by it they are distinguished from other women. It is hard to tell unmarried women and young girls from men, for they are dressed in every respect like them. The caps they have are different from those of other nations, but I am unable to describe what they are like in such a way as you would understand.

Their dwelling-places are round like tents and are made of twigs and slender sticks. At the top in the middle there is a round opening which lets in the light, and is also to enable the smoke to escape, for they always make their fire in the middle. Both the sides and the roof are covered with felt, and the doors also are made of felt. Some of these dwellings are large, others small, according to the importance or significance of the people; some can be speedily taken down and put up again and are carried on baggage animals; others cannot be taken down but are moved on carts. To carry them on a cart, for the smaller ones one ox is sufficient, for the larger ones three, four or even more according to the size. Wherever they go, be it to war or anywhere else, they always take their dwellings with them.

They are extremely rich in animals, camels, oxen, sheep, goats; they have such a number of horses and mares that I do not believe there are so many in all the rest of the world; they do not have pigs or other farm animals.

The Emperor, the nobles and other important men own large quantities of gold and silver, silk, precious stones and jewels.

* * *

They are men who are dirty in the way they take food and drink and do other things. Any evil they intend to do to others they conceal in a wonderful way so that the latter can take no precautions nor devise anything to offset their cunning. Drunkenness is considered an honourable thing by them and when anyone drinks too much, he is sick there and then, nor does this prevent him from drinking again. They are exceedingly grasping and avaricious; they are extremely exacting in their demands, most tenacious in holding on to what they have and most niggardly in giving. They consider the slaughter of other people as nothing. In short, it is impossible to put down in writing all their evil characteristics on account of the very great number of them.

Their food consists of everything that can be eaten, for they eat dogs, wolves, foxes and horses and, when driven by necessity, they feed on human flesh. For instance, when they were fighting against a city of the Kitayans, where the Emperor was residing, they besieged it for so long that they themselves completely ran out of supplies and, since they had nothing at all to eat, they thereupon took one out of every ten men for food. They eat the filth which comes away from mares when they bring forth foals. Nay, I have even seen them eating lice. They would say, "Why should I not eat them since they eat the flesh of my son and drink his blood?" I have also seen them eat mice.

They do not use table-cloths or napkins. They have neither bread nor herbs nor vegetables nor anything else, nothing but meat, of which, however, they eat so little that other people would scarcely be able to exist on it. They make their hands very dirty with the grease of the meat, but when they eat they wipe them on their leggings or the grass or some other such thing. It is the custom for the more respectable among them to have small bits of cloth with which they wipe their hands at the end when they eat meat. One of them cuts the morsels and another takes them on the point of a knife and offers them to each, to some more, to some less, according to whether they wish to show them greater or less honour. They do not wash their dishes, and, if occasionally they rinse them with the meat broth, they put it back with the meat into the pot. Pots also or spoons or other articles intended for this use, if they are cleaned at all, are washed in the same manner. They consider it a great sin if any food or drink is allowed to be wasted in any way; consequently they do not allow bones to be given to dogs until the marrow has been extracted. They do not wash their clothes nor allow them to be washed, especially from the time when thunderstorms begin until the weather changes. They drink mare's milk in very great quantities if they have it; they also drink the milk of ewes, cows, goats and even camels. They do not have wine, ale or mead unless it is sent or given to them by other nations. In the winter, moreover, unless they are wealthy, they do not have mare's milk. They boil millet in water and make it so thin that they cannot eat it but have to drink it. Each one of them drinks one or two cups in the morning and they eat nothing more during the day; in the evening, however, they are all given a little meat, and they drink the meat broth. But in the summer, seeing they have plenty of mare's milk, they seldom eat meat, unless it happens to be given to them or they catch some animal or bird when hunting.

They also have a law or custom of putting to death any man and woman they find openly committing adultery; similarly if a virgin commit fornication with anyone, they kill both the man and the woman. If anyone is found in the act of plundering or stealing in the territory under their power, he is put to death without any mercy. Again, if anyone reveals their plans, especially when they intend going to war, he is given a hundred stripes on his back, as heavy as a peasant can give with a big stick.

* * *

When they are in battle, if one or two or three or even more out of a group of ten run away, all are put to death; and if a whole group of ten flees, the rest of the group of a hundred are all put to death, if they do not flee too. In a word, unless they retreat in a body, all who take flight are put to death. Likewise if one or two or more go forward boldly to the fight, then the rest of the ten are put to death if they do not follow and, if one or more of the ten are captured, their companions are put to death if they do not rescue them.

They all have to possess the following arms at least: two or three bows, or at least one good one, three large quivers full of arrows, an axe and ropes for hauling engines of war. As for the wealthy, they have swords pointed at the end but sharp only on one side and somewhat curved, and they have a horse with armour; their legs also are covered and they have helmets and cuirasses. Some have cuirasses, and protection for their horses, fashioned out of leather in the following manner: they take strips of ox-hide, or of the skin of another animal, a hand's breadth wide and cover three or four together with pitch, and they fasten them with leather thongs or cord; in the upper strip they put the lace at one end, in the next they put it in the middle and so on to the end; consequently, when they bend, the lower strips come up over the upper ones and thus there is a double or triple thickness over the body.

They make the covering for their horses in five sections, one on one side of the horse and one on the other, and these stretch from the tail to the head and are fastened to the saddle and behind the saddle on its back and also on the neck; another section they put over its hindquarters where the ties of the two parts are fastened and in this last-named piece they make a hole for the tail to come through; covering the breast there is another section. All these pieces reach down as far as the knees or joints of the leg. On its forehead they put an iron plate which is tied to the aforementioned sections on each side of the neck.

The cuirass is made in four parts. One piece stretches from the thigh to the neck, but is shaped to fit the human figure, being narrow across the chest and curved round the body from the arms downwards; behind, over the loins, they have another piece which reaches from the neck and meets the first piece encircling the body; these two sections, namely the front one and the back, are fastened with clasps to two iron plates, one on each shoulder; also on each arm they have a piece stretching from the shoulder to the hand and open at the bottom, and on each leg another piece. All these sections are fastened together by clasps.

The upper part of the helmet is of iron or steel, but the part affording protection to the neck and throat is of leather. All these leather sections are made in the manner described above.

* * *

It should be known that when they come in sight of the enemy they attack at once, each one shooting three or four arrows at their adversaries; if they see that they are not going to be able to defeat them, they retire, going back to their own line. They do this as a blind to make the enemy follow them as far as the places where they have prepared ambushes. If the enemy pursues them to these ambushes, they surround and wound and kill them. Similarly if they see that they are opposed by a large army, they sometimes turn aside and, putting a day's or two days' journey between them, they attack and pillage another part of the country and they kill men and destroy and lay waste the land. If they perceive that they cannot even do this, then they retreat for some ten or twelve days and stay in a safe place until the army of the enemy has disbanded, whereupon they come secretly and ravage the whole land. They are indeed the most cunning in war, for they have now been fighting against other nations for forty years and more.

When however they are going to join battle, they draw up all the battle lines just as they are to fight. The chiefs or princes of the army do not take part in the fighting but take up their stand some distance away facing the enemy, and they have beside them their children on horseback and their womenfolk and horses; and sometimes they make figures of men and set them on horses. They do this to give the impression that a great crowd of fighting-men is assembled there. They send a detachment of captives and men of other nationalities who are fighting with them to meet the enemy head-on, and some Tartars may perhaps accompany them. Other columns of stronger men they dispatch far off to the right and the left so that they are not seen by the enemy and in this way they surround them and close in and so the fighting begins from all sides. Sometimes when they are few in number they are thought by the enemy, who are surrounded, to be many, especially when the latter catch sight of the children, women, horses and dummy figures described above, which are with the chief or prince of the army and which they think are combatants.

* * *

Whoever wishes to fight against the Tartars ought to have the following arms: good strong bows, crossbows, of which they are much afraid, a good supply of arrows, a serviceable axe of strong iron or a battle-axe with a long handle; the heads of the arrows for both bows and cross-bows ought to be tempered after the Tartar fashion, in salt water when they are hot, to make them hard enough to pierce the Tartar armour. They should also have swords and lances with a hook to drag the Tartars from their saddle, for they fall off very easily; knives, and cuirasses of a double thickness, for the Tartar arrows do not easily pierce such; a helmet and armour and other things to protect the body and the horses from their weapons and arrows. If there are any men not as well armed as we have described, they ought to do as the Tartars and go behind the others and shoot at the enemy with their bows and crossbows. There ought to be no stinting of money when purchasing weapons for the defence of souls and bodies and liberty and other possessions.

The army should be organised in the same way as the Tartar army, under captains of a thousand, captains of a hundred, captains of ten and the chiefs of the army. The last named ought on no account to take part in the battle, just as the Tartar chiefs take no part, but they should watch the army and direct it. They should make a law that all advance together either to battle or elsewhere in the order appointed. Severe punishment ought to be meted out to anyone who deserts another either going into battle or fighting, or takes flight when they are not retreating as a body, for if this happens a section of the Tartar force follows those fleeing and kills them with arrows while the rest fight with those who have remained on the field, and so both those who stay and those who run away are thrown into confusion and killed. Similarly anyone who turns aside to take plunder before the army of the enemy has been completely vanquished ought to be punished with a very heavy sentence; among the Tartars such a one is put to death without any mercy. The chiefs of the army should choose their battle ground, if possible a flat plain, every part of which they can watch, and if they can they should have a large forest behind them or on their flank, so situated however that the Tartars cannot come between them and the wood. The army ought not to assemble into one body, but many lines should be formed, separated from each other, only not too far apart. One line ought to be sent to meet the first line of Tartars to approach; if the Tartars feign flight they ought not to pursue them very far, certainly not further than they can see, in case the Tartars lead them into ambushes they have prepared, which is what they usually do. And let another line be in readiness to help the first if occasion require it.

Moreover they ought to have scouts in every direction, behind, to the right and to the left, to see when the other lines of Tartars are coming, and one line ought always to be sent to meet each Tartar line, for the Tartars always strive to surround their enemies; the greatest precautions ought to be taken to prevent their doing this, for in this way an army is easily vanquished. Each line should take care not to pursue them for long, on account of the ambushes they are wont to prepare, for they fight with deceit rather than courage.

The leaders of the army ought always to be ready to send help to those who are fighting if they need it. Another reason for avoiding too long a pursuit after the Tartars is so as not to tire the horses, for we have not the great quantity which they have. The horses the Tartars ride on one day they do not mount again for the next three or four days, consequently they do not mind if they tire them out seeing they have such a great number of animals. Even if the Tartars retreat our men ought not to separate from each other or be split up, for the Tartars pretend to withdraw in order to divide the army, so that afterwards they can come without any let or hindrance and destroy the whole land. The Christians should also beware of their usual tendency of over-expenditure, lest they be obliged to go home on account of lack of money and the Tartars destroy the whole earth and the name of God be blasphemed on account of their extravagance. They should take care to see that if it come to pass that some fighting men return home, others take their place.

Our leaders ought also to arrange that our army is guarded day and night, so that the Tartars do not make a sudden and unexpected attack upon them for, like the devils, they devise many ways of doing harm. Indeed our men ought to be on the alert as much during the night as in the daytime, they should never undress to lie down, nor sit at table enjoying themselves, so that they cannot be taken unawares, for the Tartars are always on the watch to see how they can inflict some damage. The inhabitants of a country who are apprehensive and fear that the Tartars are coming to attack them should have secret pits in which they should put their corn as well as other things, and this for two reasons: namely so that the Tartars cannot get hold of them and also that, if God shows them His favour, they themselves will be able to find them afterwards. If they have to flee from their country, they ought to burn the hay and straw or hide it away in a safe place so that the horses of the Tartars will find less to eat.

If they wish to fortify cities or fortresses, let them first examine them from the point of view of position, for fortified places ought to be so situated that they cannot be reduced by engines and arrows; they should have a good supply of water and wood and, if possible, it should be impossible to deprive them of an entrance and exit, and they should have sufficient inhabitants for them to take it in turns in fighting. They ought to keep a careful watch to prevent the Tartars from taking the fortress by stealth, by means of cunning. They should have sufficient supplies to last for many years, and let them keep them carefully and eat them in moderation, for they do not know how long they will have to be shut up inside their fortress. When the Tartars once begin, they lay siege to a fortress for many years, for example at the present time in the land of the Alans they have been besieging a hill for the past twelve years, the inhabitants of which have manfully resisted and killed many Tartars and nobles.

Other fortresses and cities which have not the situation described above ought to be strongly protected by means of deep, walled ditches and well-built walls and they should have a good supply of bows and arrows and slings and stones. They must take great care not to allow the Tartars to place their engines in position, but they should drive them off with their own engines. If it happen that the Tartars by some device or cunning erect their engines, then the inhabitants ought to destroy them with theirs if they can; they should also use cross-bows, slings and engines against them to prevent them from drawing near to the city. In other respects they ought to be prepared as has already been described. As for fortresses and cities situated on rivers, they should be careful to see that they cannot be flooded out. Moreover, in regard to this point it should be known that the Tartars much prefer men to shut themselves into their cities and fortresses rather than fight with them in the open, for then they say they have got their little pigs shut in their sty, and so they place men to look after them as I have told above.

If any Tartars are thrown from their horse during the battle, they ought to be taken prisoner immediately, for when they are on the ground they shoot vigorously with their arrows, wounding and killing men and horses. If they are kept they can be the means of obtaining uninterrupted peace or a large sum of money would be given for them, for they have great love for each other. As to how Tartars may be recognised, it has been told above in the place where a description is given of their appearance. When they are taken prisoner, a strict guard must be kept over them if they are to be prevented from escaping. There are men of many other nations with them and these can be distinguished from them by means of the description set down above. It is important to know that there are many men in the Tartar army who, if they saw their opportunity and could rely on our men not to kill them, would fight against the Tartars in every part of the army, as they themselves told us, and they would do them worse harm than those who are their declared enemies.

Christopher Dawson, ed., *Mission to Asia* (New York: Sheed and Ward, 1955), 7, 16–17, 33–34, 36, 46–49.

DISCUSSION QUESTIONS

1. Why were Mongol clothing and housing so seemingly simple?
2. Why were Mongols so unselective in consumption of food?
3. What made the Mongols such a formidable fighting force?
4. Why does John of Plano Carpini focus so much on the Mongol military?

Marignolli's Recollections of Eastern Travel

John of Marignolli (born before 1290), a bishop descended from an elite family in Florence, was at the papal court in Avignon at a critical juncture. In 1338, a delegation from the Mongol domains in China arrived to report that John of Monte Corvino, the papal legate to China, had died eight years earlier and the Christian population there had had no spiritual leader since that time. Pope Innocent VI responded by dispatching an embassy of fifty friars, including John of Marignolli, to cater to the spiritual needs of this Christian population. John and the other members of the group first met and spent time with Özbeg, the khan of the Golden Horde, who had converted to Islam. His fine treatment of the Christian travelers confirms the Mongols' repeated proclamations of religious toleration. John and his delegation then pressed forward, reaching China in 1342. They ingratiated themselves with Togh Temür, the Great Khan and the last Yuan dynasty emperor, by offering war horses as well as lavish gifts from the Pope. In turn, Togh Temür earned John's praise for his hospitality and his gracious treatment of the Western envoys. John remained in China for five years and then spent six years traveling through Southeast Asia and the Middle East before returning to Avignon in 1353.

He returned with a letter from the Great Khan and a somewhat disorganized report. His account consisted of a truncated narrative of his adventures and lengthy descriptions of Paradise and other Christian conceptions. This unusual text, a mixture of several genres, does, however, reveal that even the last Yuan dynasty rulers welcomed contacts with other parts of the world.

We set out from Avignon in the month of December, came to Naples in the beginning of Lent, and stopped there till Easter (which fell at the end of March), waiting for a ship of Genoa, which was coming with the Tartar envoys whom the Kaan had sent from his great city of Cambalec to the Pope, to request the latter to despatch an embassy to his court, whereby communication might be established, and a treaty of alliance struck between him and the Christians; for he greatly loves and honours our faith. Moreover the chief princes of his whole empire, more than thirty thousand in number, who are called Alans, and govern the whole Orient, are Christians either in fact or in name, calling themselves *the Pope's slaves*, and ready to die for the *Franks*. For so they term us, not indeed from France, but from Frankland. Their first apostle was Friar John, called De Monte Corvino, who seventy-two years previously, after having been soldier, judge, and doctor in the service of the Emperor Frederic, had become a Minor Friar, and a most wise and learned one.

Howbeit on the first of May we arrived by sea at Constantinople, and stopped at Pera till the feast of St. John Baptist. We had no idle time of it however, for we were engaged in a most weighty controversy with the Patriarch of the Greeks and their whole Council in the palace of St. Sophia. And there God wrought in us a new miracle, giving us a mouth and wisdom which they were not able to resist; for they were constrained to confess that they must needs be schismatics, and had no plea to urge against their own condemnation except the intolerable arrogance of the Roman prelates.

Thence we sailed across the Black Sea, and in eight days arrived at Caffa, where there are Christians of many sects. From that place we went on to the first Emperor of the Tartars, Usbec, and laid before him the letters which we bore, with certain pieces of cloth, a great war-horse, some strong liquor, and the Pope's presents. And after the winter was over, having been well fed, well clothed, loaded with handsome presents, and supplied by the King with horses and travelling expenses, we proceeded to Armalec [the capital] of the Middle Empire. There we built a church, bought a piece of ground, dug wells, sung masses and baptized several; preaching freely and openly, notwithstanding the fact that only the year before the Bishop and six other Minor Friars had there undergone for Christ's sake a glorious martyrdom, illustrated by brilliant miracles. The names of these martyrs were Friar Richard the Bishop, a Burgundian by nation, Friar Francis of Alessandria, Friar Paschal of Spain (this one was a prophet and saw the heavens open, and foretold the martyrdom which should befall him and his brethren, and the overthrow of the Tartars of Saray by a flood, and the destruction of Armalec in vengeance for their martyrdom, and that the Emperor would be slain on the third day after their martyrdom, and many other glorious things); Friar Laurence of Ancona, Friar Peter, an Indian friar who acted as their interpreter, and Gillott [Gilottus], a merchant.

Towards the end of the third year after our departure from the Papal Court, quitting Armalec we came to the Cyollos Kagon, i.e. to the Sand Hills thrown up by the wind. Before the days of the Tartars nobody believed that the earth was habitable beyond these, nor indeed was it believed that there was any country at all beyond. But the Tartars by God's permission, and with wonderful exertion, did cross them, and found themselves in what the philosophers call the torrid and impassable zone. Pass it however the Tartars did; and so did I, and that twice. 'Tis of this that David speaketh in the Psalms, '*Posuit desertum,*' &c. After having passed it we came to Cambalec, the chief seat of the Empire of the East. Of its incredible magnitude, population, and military array, we will say nothing. But the Grand Kaam, when he beheld the great horses, and the Pope's presents, with his letter, and King Robert's too, with their golden seals, and when he saw us also, rejoiced greatly, being delighted, yea exceedingly delighted with everything, and treated us with the greatest honour. And when I entered the Kaam's presence it was in full festival vestments, with a very fine cross carried before me, and candles and incense, whilst *Credo in Unum Deum* was chaunted, in that glorious palace where he dwells. And when the chaunt was ended I bestowed a full benediction, which he received with all humility.

And so we were dismissed to one of the Imperial apartments which had been most elegantly fitted up for us; and two princes were appointed to attend to all our wants. And this they did in the most liberal manner, not merely as regards meat and drink, but even down to such things as paper for lanterns, whilst all necessary servants also were detached from the Court to wait upon us. And so they tended us for nearly four years, never failing to treat us with unbounded respect. And I should add that they kept us and all our establishment clothed in costly raiment. And considering that we were thirty-two persons, what the Kaam expended for everything on our account must have amounted, as well as I can calculate, to more than four thousand marks. And we had many and glorious disputations with the Jews and other sectaries; and we made also a great harvest of souls in that empire.

Henry Yule, *Cathay and the Way Thither*, new ed. by Henri Cordier (London: Hakluyt Society, 1913–16), 210–14.

DISCUSSION QUESTIONS

1. How does John of Marignolli's account attest to the Mongol era as the beginning of intercultural and global relations?
2. What prompted the Mongol khan to offer such a warm welcome to European missionaries?

Kirakos of Ganjak, On the Mongols

Kirakos of Ganjak (1201–1272) wrote a history of Armenia that covered the era, his own, when the Mongols controlled Armenia. Tutored in a cave by a renowned teacher, he was well versed in Armenian history. His studies were interrupted by the arrival of the Mongol invaders, who captured him and his teacher. He managed to escape after a few months and returned to teaching and research for the remainder of his life. The most notable event in his later life was a 1255 audience with King Hetum I of Armenia, who had just returned from Möngke (r. 1251–59) Khan's court in Mongolia.

His History of Armenia *revealed his erudition. The section on the Mongols was particularly well informed because Kirakos had been an eyewitness to the attacks and rule. However, his narrative and account naturally tended to reflect his own views on the Mongols.*

When the occasion offered they ate continually and drank insatiably; when it did not, they were abstemious. They ate all living creatures, clean and unclean, and they most esteemed the flesh of the horse, cutting it limb from limb and boiling or roasting it without salt; then they carved it up small, soaked it in salt water and ate it thus. Some of them ate kneeling, like camels, and some sitting, and when eating they shared alike between masters and servants. And when drinking *γmuz* and wine one of them took it into his hands in a large vessel and having drawn some out in a small cup scattered it skywards and then to the east and west and south and north; and then he that scattered it having drunk a little of it offered it to the most senior person. And if anyone brought them food or drink they first caused the bearer to eat or drink it and then ate or drank it themselves, lest they might be deceived by some deadly poison.

They took as many wives as they liked, but they in no way spared adulterers with their wives, though they themselves had commerce with strange women indiscriminately wherever they found them. And they detested theft to such an extent that they punished it with a most evil death.

And they had no religion or form of worship, but they used continually to mention the name of God. Whether they thanked the Being of God or called someone else God, we do not know nor did they themselves. But usually they said this, that their king was related to God, God having taken the heavens as His share and given the earth to the Xaγan; for they said that Cangz Γan, the father of the Xaγan, was not born of the seed of man, but a light came from the unseen and entered through the skylight of the house and said to his mother: "Conceive and thou shalt give birth to a son [who shall be] emperor of the earth." And by this [light], they said, she bore him.

This was told us by Grigor the *isxan*, the son of Marzpan, the brother of Aslanbeg, Sargis and Amira, of the family of the Mamikonians, who had heard it from a great man from amongst the great commanders, whose name was Γut'un Nuin, one day when he was instructing young children.

And when anyone of them died or was put to death, sometimes they carried him around with them for many days, because a devil had entered him and was uttering many idle things; and sometimes they burnt him, and sometimes they buried him in a deep grave, and with him they laid his arms and clothing, and gold and silver, and whatever belonged to him. And if it was one of their great men, they laid some of his men-servants and maid-servants with him in the tomb, because, they said, they might wait on him, and also a horse, because, they said, there would be fierce fighting there. And when they wished to have a memorial of the dead man, they ripped open the belly of a horse and pulled out all the flesh without bones, and then they burnt the intestines and bones and sewed up the skin of the horse as though it had its whole body. Having sharpened a great pole they thrust it in the belly and pulled it out through the mouth; and thus they raised it up on a tree or some elevated place.

John Boyle, "Kirakos of Ganjak on the Mongols," *Central Asiatic Journal* 8 (1963): 201–04, 207.

DISCUSSION QUESTIONS

1. How would a reader of Kirakos's report view the Mongols?
2. How would a reader be able to determine its reliability?
3. What does Kirakos's description of the Mongols' burial practices reveal about their religion and their conception of death?

Part III
Life and Conquests of Chinggis Khan

The Secret History of the Mongols

The Secret History of the Mongols, *a semi-fictional and semi-factual account, is the only extant Mongol primary source of the thirteenth century. Composed some years after Chinggis Khan's death in the only just developed Uyghur script of Mongolian, the original text was lost, and only a Chinese transcription, not a translation, of the work has survived. Since its discovery in the late nineteenth century, the* Secret History *has been translated into a wide variety of languages, including Russian, French, German, Japanese, Hungarian, and English. The English translation presented below treats the work as a poem and emphasizes its literary quality.*

The Secret History *starts with a description of the Mongol ancestors and then focuses on Chinggis Khan's early life, his conflicts with other Mongol leaders, his unification of the Mongols, his military campaigns beyond Mongolia, and his death; it winds up with a brief consideration of his son Ögödei's reign. It offers a vivid and colorful account of early Mongol history, with explanations of social relations and traditional customs and with compelling portraits of the leading figures, including Chinggis's competitors. The author has himself composed speeches for the important characters; he obviously was not present when such conversations took place. Although the author often depicts Chinggis in a heroic light, he does not shy away from exposing the Mongol leader's flaws and misbehavior. For example, in this selection, he shows Chinggis killing his half-brother.*

What does this good omen mean?' I asked.
My friend Yesugei,
I had this dream the very moment you were leading your son to our camp.
What could it mean?
Obviously it was a sign that a nobleman like yourself would come to our camp.
Since the days of old we Ungirad have been protected by the beauty of our daughters,
by the loveliness of our granddaughters,
and so we've stayed out of battles and wars.
When you elect a new khan,
we take our loveliest daughters and place them on carts.
Harnessing a black camel to the cart,
we have him trot off to the khan's tent.
We offer our daughters to sit there beside him and be his khatun.
We don't challenge empires;
we don't go to war with our neighbors.
We just bring up our daughters and place them in the front of the carts.
Harnessing a black camel to the cart,
we lead them off to the khan's tent.
We offer our daughters to sit by the khan,
and he places them up on the throne.
Since the days of old the Ungirad have had khatun as their shields.
We've survived by the loveliness of our granddaughters,
by the beauty of our daughters.
When one of our boys wants to marry
you can judge the wealth of our camp to decide if you want him.
But as for our girls you only have to look at their beauty.
My friend Yesugei, let's go to my tent.
I've got a young daughter there.
My friend should meet her."
Dei the Wise led Yesugei's horse to his tent and helped him dismount.
When Yesugei saw Dei's daughter he was impressed.
She was a girl whose face filled with light,

whose eyes filled with fire,
and he began to consider her father's proposal.
She was ten years old, a year older than Temujin,
and her name was Borte.
After spending the night in the tent,
the next morning Yesugei asked Dei for his daughter.
"I could let you have her after awhile,
waiting for you to ask me again and again,
but who'd praise me for stalling?
I could let you have her right away,
just waiting for you to ask me twice,
and who'd curse me for replying too quick?
No, this girl's fate is not to grow old by the door of the tent she was
born in.
I'll be happy to give you my daughter.
But now you should go,
and leave your son with me for awhile,
so we can get to know our new son-in-law."
Both men gave their pledge to the other
and Yesugei added:
"I'll leave you my son for awhile.
You should know that he's frightened by dogs.
Don't let the dogs frighten him, my friend."
Then Yesugei offered his lead horse as a gift,
and leaving Temujin in Dei's tent, he rode back to his people.

As he rode back Yesugei came on a camp of the Tatar,
who were feasting below Mount Chegcher on the Yellow Steppe.
Tired and thirsty, he dismounted to join in the feasting.
But the Tatar recognized who he was, and said to themselves:
"Yesugei of the Kiyan clan is among us here."
They remembered the times he'd defeated them in battle.
Secretly they decided to kill him,
mixing poisons into the drinks he was offered.
On his way back he felt something was wrong
and after riding three days to get back to his tent
he knew he was dying.
Yesugei the Brave spoke from his bed, saying:

"I feel that I'm dying.
Who's here beside me?"
Someone answered him:
"Munglig, the son of Old Man Charakha is here."
Yesugei called the boy over to him and said:
"Munglig, my child, my sons are still very young.
As I rode back from leaving Temujin with his wife's family
I was secretly poisoned by the Tatar.
I can feel that I'm dying now.
Take care of my sons like they were your own little brothers.
Take care of my wife like she was your own elder sister.
Go quickly now, Munglig, my child, and bring Temujin back."
Then Yesugei passed away.
Following Yesugei's last words Munglig went to Dei the Wise and said:
"My Elder Brother Yesugei's heart aches
and he is constantly thinking of his son.
I've come to take Temujin back to him."
Dei the Wise answered him:
"If my friend thinks so much of his son, I'll let him go.
When he's seen his father again, have him quickly come back."
So Father Munglig brought Temujin back to his family.

The following spring Ambaghai's widows, Orbei and Sokhatai,
the senior women of the Tayichigud clan,
performed the ceremony of sacrifice to the ancestor's spirits.
By the time Hogelun Ujin arrived for the service
they'd already burnt all the meat
and divided it between them, leaving her nothing.
Hogelun said to them:
"You must be saying to yourselves,
'Yesugei the Brave is dead now and his sons are still boys.'
So you think you can just leave me out of the ceremony
and keep it all for yourselves?
You think you can divide up the meats and leave nothing for me?
I see what you're up to.
You think that I'll just sit here while you're feasting from now on,
that you don't even have to invite me to join you.

And one morning you'll break camp and move on,
and not even wake me."
Orbei and Sokhatai, the two old khatun, answered her:
"Obviously you live by some rule that says,
'I don't need to be offered some food before I take something to eat.'
You have the custom of eating whatever you can find.
You seem to have a rule that says,
'I don't need to be invited to take part in a feast.'
Your custom is to just come uninvited and take for yourself.
Tell us, Hogelun, do you say to yourself,
'Ambaghai Khan is dead now,'
is that why you think you can insult us this way?"
Later the old women conferred among themselves and said:
"The best thing to do is abandon these people,
these mothers and sons.
We should break camp and leave them behind."

So at dawn the next day the two chiefs of the Tayichigud clan,
Targhutai Kiriltugh and Todogen Girte,
ordered the people to move on down the Onan River.
Old Man Charakha saw they were leaving Hogelun Ujin behind,
that they were abandoning these mothers and sons,
so he stepped forward, protesting to Todogen Girte.
But Todogen said to him:
"Everything has changed now.
The deepest waters are dry,
the brightest gem has been broken to pieces,"
and the chief ordered the people to keep moving along.
Then when Old Man Charakha turned away from him
Todogen yelled back:
"What gives you the right to say that we're wrong to do this?"
and he drove a spear into the old man's back.
Old Man Charakha struggled back to his tent
and lay down in great pain from his wound.
Temujin came to his bedside and the old man said to him:
"As the Tayichigud were taking the people your good father assembled,

as they were taking our people away from the camp,
I stepped out and protested to Todogen.
See what he's done to me."
Temujin sat and wept by the dying man
and then left the tent.
When Hogelun Ujin saw the people were leaving her
she grabbed up the standard of Yesugei the Brave
and rode out into the travelling camp.
Just the sight of her holding the banner
and shouting caused half of the people to stop and turn back with her.
But the ones who turned back couldn't stay.
They were forced to return with the others by the Tayichigud
and told to move on.
After the Tayichigud brothers had abandoned the old camp,
leaving only Hogelun Ujin,
her sons and her little ones,
after the Tayichigud had taken all of the people away,
leaving only the mothers and sons,
Hogelun Ujin, a woman born with great power,
took care of her sons.
Proudly she put on her headdress and gathered the folds of her skirt.
She went up and down the banks of the Onan
and gathered pears and wild fruit.
Day and night she found food for their mouths.
Mother Hogelun, a woman born with great courage,
took care of her sons.
Taking a juniper stick in her hands
she fed them by digging up roots.
These boys who were nourished on the wild onion and pear,
who were fed by Ujin, the Mother,
became the great Lords of all men.
These boys who lived on the roots that she dug for them,
who were cared for with pride by Mother Ujin,
became the wise men who gave us our laws.
These boys who were nourished on the wild onion and pear,
who were fed by the beautiful Ujin,

grew up to be fine, daring men.
Once they'd grown into men,
they pledged to themselves: "Now we'll feed our mother."
They sat on the banks of the Mother Onan
and bent needles they'd found into fishhooks.
With these hooks they caught a few misshapen fish.
They made nets to sweep through the river
and they caught tiny fish.
With these in their turn they helped feed their mother.

One day Temujin and Khasar,
along with their half-brothers Begter and Belgutei,
were sitting together on the riverbank
pulling a hook through the water
when they saw a shiny fish had been caught on it.
When they landed the fish
Begter and Belgutei took it away from Temujin and Khasar.
Temujin and Khasar ran back to their tent to complain to Mother
Ujin:
"Begter and Belgutei took a fish from us,
a shiny fish that bit on our hook."
But even though Begter and Belgutei were only her stepsons
Mother Ujin replied:
"Stop this!
How can brothers act this way with each other?
Now, when we've no one to fight beside us but our own shadows,
when there's nothing to whip our horses but their own tails,
how will we get our revenge on the Tayichigud brothers?
Why do you fight among yourselves like the five sons of Mother
Alan?
Don't be this way."
But Temujin and Khasar wouldn't listen to what she said.
They ignored her warning and answered instead:
"Besides that, yesterday they took a bird from us,
a lark we'd shot down with one of our own arrows.
And now they've stolen a fish.
How can we live with them?"
The two boys pushed aside the door of the tent and stalked out.

While Begter sat in a clearing watching the family's nine horses grazing,
Temujin hid himself in the grass and crept up from behind
while Khasar crept up from the front.
Then suddenly they sprang up,
drawing their arrows to shoot,
and Begter, seeing what they meant to do to him, said:
"How can you do this to me,
when our mouths are filled
with the bitterness of what the Tayichigud clan has done,
when we ask ourselves,
'How can we get our revenge on them?'
how can you treat me like some dirt in your eye,
like something that's keeping the food from your mouth?
How can you do this,
when there's no one to fight beside us but our own shadows,
when there's nothing to whip our horses but their own tails,
how can you kill me?
But if you must
don't destroy the fire of my hearth.
Don't kill my brother Belgutei too!"
Then Begter sat down before them,
crossing his legs,
and waited to see what they'd do to him.
At close range both Temujin and Khasar shot arrows into him,
striking him down in the front and the back,
and then left him.
When they got back to the tent
Mother Ujin could see on their faces what they'd done.
She looked at her two sons,
then pointing first at Temujin said to them:
"Killers, both of you!
When he came out screaming from the heat of my womb
this one was born holding a clot of black blood in his hand.
And now you've both destroyed without thinking,
like the Khasar dog who eats its own afterbirth,
like the panther that heedlessly leaps from a cliff,
like the lion who can't control its own fury,

like the python that thinks: 'I'll swallow my prey alive,'
like the falcon that foolishly dives at its own shadow,
like the river pike who silently swallows the smaller fish,
like the he-camel who snaps at the heels of his colt,
like the wolf who hides himself in the blizzard to hunt down his prey,
like the mandarin duck who eats his own chicks when they fall behind,
like the jackal who fights with anyone who's touched him,
like the tiger who doesn't think before seizing his prey,
you've killed your own brother!

* * *

The Wars in Mongolia

Temujin and Jamugha pitched their tents in the Khorkonagh Valley.
With their people united in one great camp,
the two leaders decided they should renew their friendship,
their pledge of anda.
They remembered when they'd first made that pledge,
and said, "We should love one another again."
That first time they'd met Temujin was eleven years old.
In those days
when he and his family had been abandoned by the Tayichigud,
he'd first met Jamugha,
a young noble of the Jadaran clan,
and they'd played at games of knucklebone dice on the banks of the Onan,
casting bones on the frozen waters of the Onan.
Jamugha had given Temujin the knucklebone of a roebuck
and in return Temujin gave Jamugha a knucklebone of brass.
With that exchange the two boys had pledged themselves anda forever.
Then later that spring
when the two were off in the forest together shooting arrows,
Jamugha took two pieces of calf-horn.
He bored holes in them,

glued them together to fashion a whistling arrowhead,
and he gave this arrow as a present to Temujin.
In return Temujin gave him a beautiful arrow with a cypresswood tip.
With that exchange of arrows
they declared themselves anda a second time.
So Temujin and Jamugha said to each other:
"We've heard the elders say,
'When two men become anda their lives become one.
One will never desert the other and will always defend him.'

***

He rode up to the cart where Mother Hogelun was riding
and said to her:
"Anda Jamugha said to me,
'Let's pitch our camp near the mountains.
Let the cattle herders make a camp for themselves.
Let's pitch our camp near the stream.
Let the shepherds look for their own food.'
I did not understand what he meant so I said nothing.
I've come to you thinking,
'I'll ask my mother if she knows what he means.'"
Before Mother Hogelun could answer
Borte Ujin spoke up, saying:
"They say Anda Jamugha's a fickle man.
I think the time's come when he's finally grown tired of us.
These words are meant to cover some kind of plot.
When he stops, let's not pitch our camp.
Let's tell our people to keep right on moving,
and if we travel all night
by daybreak our camps will be well separated."

Agreeing with what Borte Ujin had said,
when Jamugha stopped to pitch camp
Temujin ordered his people to keep moving,
and they drove their carts on through the night.
As they travelled Temujin's people passed by the Tayichigud camp.
When the Tayichigud heard them approaching

they fled from their camp toward the place Jamugha had pitched his tents.
When Temujin's people reached the camp the Tayichigud had abandoned
they found a young boy named Kokochu who'd been left behind
and they gave him to Mother Hogelun.
From that time on
Mother Hogelun took care of him.

* * *

When I heard that my father the Khan was in such a condition
I remembered the fact that you had declared yourself anda with my father
and I sent messengers to meet you,
then came back to meet you myself at Lake Gusegur.
I gathered taxes from my people and gave them to you,
remembering that you were my father's anda.
Isn't this why we declared ourselves father and son in the Black Forest by the Tula?
I took you into my camp circle and cared for you that winter
and in the fall when we attacked Toghtoga Beki and defeated him
I took all their herds, their grain, and their palace tents
and presented them to my father the Khan.
There wasn't a day I allowed you to go hungry.
There wasn't a month you weren't given the things that you needed.
Then we went to war against Buyirugh Khan of the Naiman
and followed him over the Altai,
from Ulugh Tagh down the Urunggu River Valley,
destroying his forces at Lake Kishil Bashi.
As we returned we met with Kogsegu Sabragh,
who'd gathered an army of Naiman to fight us in the Bayidaragh Valley.
Since it was already evening
we agreed to spend the night there, saying,
"We'll fight in the morning."
Then you, my father the Khan,
lit fires at your battle stations

and moved your army away up the Khara Segul under cover of darkness.
Early the next morning I saw you had left,
and saying "They treat us like we were burnt meat left from a sacrifice,"
I took my people out the Eter Valley,
over the Altai to the Donkey-back Steppe.
And Kogsegu Sabragh came after you
and took the wives and sons of Senggum,
took half of the people,
the herds, and the provisions of my father the Khan.
And Toghtoga Beki's two sons escaped from you,
and took all their people back to rejoin their father at Barghujin.
Then you, my father the Khan, said to me,
"Kogsegu Sabragh has taken my people.
My son, send me your four heroes."
I didn't act the way you had acted toward me.
I sent you my soldiers, led by my four heroes,
Bogorchu, Mukhali, Boroghul, and Chilagun the Brave.
Senggum's horse had been killed by an arrow
and the Naiman were about to take him when my four heroes arrived.
They saved him,
they saved all his sons and his wives.
And then, my father the Khan, you said to me,
"My people and possessions have been saved for me,
saved by my son, Temujin, and his four heroes."
Now my father the Khan,
what reason do you have to complain against me?
Send me a messenger stating what offense I've committed against you.'"
When Ong Khan heard these words he cried:
"Ah, what have I done?
Should I divide myself from my son?
If I do I divide myself from my solemn promises.
Should I ignore what he's said to me?
If I do I ignore my own obligations."
He paused and they could see he was deeply troubled.

When he spoke again, he swore an oath, saying:
"When I see my son,
if I harbor any evil against him
may my blood flow like this,"
and taking a knife used to sharpen arrows,
he cut the tip of his little finger.
The blood from the cut filled a small birch-bark cup
which he gave to the messengers, saying:
"Give this to my son."

* * *

When Chingis Khan defeated the Naiman army
Jamugha had been with the Naiman
and in the battle all of his people were taken away.
He had escaped with only five followers
and became a bandit in the Tangnu Mountains.
One day he and his companions were lucky enough to kill a great mountain sheep,
and as they sat around the fire roasting the mutton
Jamugha said to his companions:
"What nobleman's sons are so lucky today
to have such a feast of roast mutton to eat?"
But even as he said this
his five followers seized him,
and binding Jamugha they brought him to Chingis Khan.
Because he'd been captured this way, Jamugha said:
"Tell my anda, the Khan,
'Black crows have captured a beautiful duck.
Peasants and slaves have laid hands on their lord.
My anda the Khan will see this and know what to do.
Brown vultures have captured a mandarin duck.
Slaves and servants have conspired against their lord.
Surely my holy anda will know how to respond to this.'"
When he heard Jamugha's words Chingis Khan made a decree:
"How can we allow men who lay hands on their own lord to live?
Who could trust people like this?
Such people should be killed
along with all their descendants!"

He brought before Jamugha the men who had seized him,
these men who had betrayed their own lord,
and in their lord's presence their heads were cut off.
Then Chingis Khan said:
'Tell Jamugha this.
Now we two are together.
Let's be allies.
Once we moved together like the two shafts of a cart,
but you thought about separating from me and you left.
Now that we're together again in one place
let's each be the one to remind the other of what he forgot;
let's each be the one to awaken the other's judgment whenever it sleeps.
Though you left me you were always my anda.
On the day when we met on the battlefield
the thought of trying to kill me brought pain to your heart.
Even though you went your own way
the day when we met as enemies in war
the thought that I would die brought you pain.
If you ask me, "When did this happen?"
I'll tell you it was when I met the Kereyid at the sands of Khalakhaljid.
You sent me a messenger
to inform me about what you'd said to our father, Ong Khan.
That was the service you did for me there.
Then again when we fought with the Naiman
you sent me a messenger telling me how you'd terrified the Naiman.
They were killed by your mouth;
your words made them die.
You told me their own fear would kill them.
That was the service you did for me there.'"
Jamugha answered him:
"Long ago when we were children in the Khorkhonagh Valley
I declared myself to be your anda.
Together we ate the food which is never digested
and spoke words to each other which are never forgotten,
and at night we shared one blanket to cover us both.

Then it was as if people came between us with knives,
slashing our legs and stabbing our sides,
and we were separated from each other.
I thought to myself,
'We've made solemn promises to each other'
and my face was so blackened by the winds of shame
that I couldn't bring myself to show my face,
this shameful windburned face,
before the warm face of my anda, the Khan.
I thought to myself,
'We've spoken words to each other that are never forgotten'
and my face was so red from the heat of my shame
that I went far away from you,
unable to show this burned, peeling face
before the clear face of my anda, whose memory is long.
And now my anda, the Khan wants to favor me,
and says to me, 'Let's be allies.'
When I should have been his ally I deserted him.
Now, my anda, you've pacified every nation;
you've united every tribe in the world.
The Great Khan's throne has given itself to you.
Now that the world is ready for you
what good would I be as your ally?
I'd only invade your dreams in the dark night
and trouble your thoughts in the day.
I'd be like a louse on your collar,
like a thorn under your shirt.
I was brought up by my father's grandmothers.
I went wrong when I strove to be a better man than my anda.
In this life, of the two of us,
it's my name that's reached from sunrise to sunset;
it's Jamugha who's reached the end of his days.
My anda has a wise mother.
Having been born a great hero,
he has skillful young brothers.
Having many fine men by his side,
he's always been greater than I am.
As for me,

since I lost both my parents when I was young,
I have no younger brothers.
My wife is a babbling fool.
I can't trust the men at my side.
Because of all this
my anda, whose destiny is Heaven's will,
has surpassed me in everything.
My anda, if you want to favor me,
then let me die quickly and you'll be at peace with your heart.
When you have me killed, my anda,
see that it's done without shedding my blood.
Once I am dead and my bones have been buried high on a cliff
I will protect your seed and the seed of your seed.
I will become a prayer to protect you.
My very nature is different than yours.
I've been crushed by my anda's generosity and greatness.
Remember these words that I've spoken
and repeat them to each other morning and night.
Now let me die quickly."
Hearing this Chingis Khan spoke:
"Though my anda deserted me
and said many things against me,
I've never heard that he ever wanted me dead.
He's a man we all might learn from
but he's not willing to stay with us.
If I simply ordered him to be killed
there isn't a diviner in the world who could justify it.
If I harmed this man's life without good reason
it would bring a curse on us.
Jamugha is a noble and important man.
You can speak to him and give him this reason.
Tell him,
'One time in the past
because Jochi Darmala and Taichar stole a herd of horses from one another,
Anda Jamugha, you broke your oath
and attacked me at Seventy Marshes.
I was forced to run from you there,

retreating to the refuge of Jerene Narrows.
That time you put fear in my heart.
Now I say "Let's be allies" but you refuse me.
When I try to spare your life you won't allow it.'
So speak to Jamugha and tell him,
'Allow this man to kill you
according to your own wishes,
without shedding your blood.'"
And Chingis Khan made a decree, saying:
"Execute Jamugha without shedding his blood
and bury his bones with all due honor."
He had Jamugha killed and his bones properly buried.

The Secret History of the Mongols, translated by Paul Kahn (San Francisco: North Point Press, 1984), 15–22, 44, 46, 92–93, 120–24.

DISCUSSION QUESTIONS

1. Drawing on the Ungirad chief's speech, describe conditions among the Mongols before Chinggis Khan's rise to power.
2. Describe the position of women based on the accounts of Hogelun, Chinggis Khan's mother.
3. What do Chinggis's murder of his half-brother and his mother's reaction to such intrafamily violence reveal about Mongol values?
4. What do Chinggis's relations with Jamukha and the Ong Khan reveal about unity among the Mongols at this time in history?
5. Analyze the concept of loyalty among the Mongols.

Rashid al-Din, Compendium of Chronicles

A Jewish physician who converted to Islam in his thirties, Rashid al-Din (ca. 1247–1317) was the quintessential Renaissance man. After a brief career as a doctor, he impressed the Mongol overlords of the Middle East and was recruited, possibly as a steward to one of the Il-Khans. He rose rapidly in government, eventually reaching the highest position of vizier. During the era of the Il-Khan

Ghazan (r. 1295–1304), he played a vital role in introducing economic reforms designed to benefit the native population, not simply the Mongols, and to foster the interests of peasants and merchants. His success translated into positions of governors for eight of his sons and the establishment in the Il-Khanate capital of Tabriz of his own endowment, which housed a mosque, a hospital, and other public buildings. Here and in other locations throughout the Mongol domains, he developed his wide-ranging interests in everything from agriculture to the arts. Like nearly all the Il-Khanate's viziers, he met an untimely death. With power came enemies, one of whom accused him of poisoning the Il-Khan Öljeitü (r. 1304–1316) and had him executed.

His reputation rests on his Compendium of Chronicles. *Ghazan Khan, concerned that the Mongols in the Middle East would lose touch with their heritage, commissioned him to write a history of the Mongols. Gathering around him informants, assistants, and texts, Rashid al-Din started with that assignment but eventually enlarged it to include histories of Iran, the Muslim world, China, India, the Franks, and others. In short, he wrote the first world history and provided funds to his endowment for illustrations as well as for an annual copying in Persian and Arabic of his work.*

We say, therefore—and success is through God—that Genghis Khan was orphaned of his father in childhood at the age of thirteen. When the many tribes that had previously gathered obediently around his father, Yesügäi Bahadur, saw Genghis Khan as a mere child, they abandoned him. Since his mother, Ö'älün Ekä, was extremely competent and intelligent, she preserved and protected him and the followers and soldiers left by Yesügäi Bahadur. Many times Genghis Khan experienced setbacks, and several times the Tayichi'ut clans seized the opportunity to take him prisoner, but God delivered him from the brink of death. Inasmuch as it had been God's will from all eternity that he become ruler of the world, he gradually grew in strength until, by virtue of painful labors and having forbearance in the face of great obstacles, he was able to bear difficult tasks with patience so that when he attained rule and ease he was able to appreciate such a great good thing and be grateful, and also so that when he reached lofty heights he was capable of keeping every person in the world in his proper place.

Despite his setbacks and the multiplicity of difficulties, he was magnificently brave and courageous as well as extremely intelligent, skilled, farsighted, and cultured. His name and reputation for generosity and beneficence spread in all directions, affection for him appeared in all natures, and nations inclined to him so that he grew strong and mighty and rendered his friends victorious and prosperous and his enemies vanquished and despised. He often quarreled with and suffered various torments from his and his father's relatives and cousins because they were envious of him, particularly the tribes of the Tayichi'ut, who were neighbors and whose *yurts* were nearby. It was more important to deal militarily with them than with those who were unrelated and separated by greater distances. Finally he conquered that nation and brought those who remained under the yoke of subjugation, as will be described. After that, a tribe of his relatives united with Ong Khan, the ruler of the Kerayit with whom Genghis Khan had a long-standing friendship and father-son relationship, and planned to assassinate him. Since their dwelling place and *yurts* were near and contiguous with his, it was necessary to launch a campaign against them. Many battles were fought until Genghis Khan finally conquered and annihilated them.

* * *

The Beginning of the Friendship between Genghis Khan and Ong Khan

This came about as follows. Because they were neighbors, there was a long-standing friendship and alliance between Genghis Khan's father, Yesügäi Bahadur, and Ong Khan. During hard times Yesügäi Bahadur helped Ong Khan and rescued him from the brink of disaster. They called each other *anda*. As the proverb says, "Love is inherited," so Genghis Khan continued in the path of affection and called [Ong Khan] "father." Ong Khan was the ruler of the Kerayit and Tonqayit nation and of other tribes who were in the Kerayit [confederation]. They constituted a large people and a numerous army, and their ancient rulers were renowned. They bore a resemblance to the Mongol clans, and their manners and customs, as well as dialect and language, were close to each other's.

* * *

Jamuqa Goes to Ong Khan's Son Sangun and Causes Him to Break with Genghis Khan; They and Other Tribes Ally, and Genghis Khan Does Battle with Them in Qalajin Älät

Since Jamuqa Sächän was basically jealous of and malevolent toward Genghis Khan, as well as being treacherous and evil, he now went to Sangun and said, "My elder brother Genghis Khan is in cahoots with Tayang Khan, who is your enemy. He is constantly sending envoys to him." He insinuated this thought into Sangun's mind, and he was so gullible he thought it was true and made a pact with Jamuqa, saying, "When Genghis Khan mounts, our soldiers will come in from the flanks and attack him."

As has been mentioned, since Genghis Khan's uncle Daritai Otchigin and his cousins Qutula Qa'an's son Altan and Näkün Taishi's son Quchar had been angered by Genghis Khan over the matter of the booty he had taken from them when they broke their word during the battle with the Tatar, they too joined the conspiracy. Taghai Qulatai of the Mangqut and Moqur Qauran, the leader of the Hadargin clan of the Niru'un, also conspired with this group to attack Genghis Khan.

Sangun had then decamped and was headed, separately from his father, to a place called Älät. He sent one of his commanders, Sayiqan Tödä'än by name, as a messenger to his father to make it so that Genghis Khan and his soldiers would mingle with Sangun and his men when they camped, thus giving him a chance to attack. He took counsel with Jamuqa, who called Sangun *anda* and was *anda* to Genghis Khan. Through the above-mentioned messenger he sent a message saying, "This man who claims to be your friend and supporter, the son of Ö'älün Ekä (meaning Genghis Khan), has contemplated such treachery. We are considering making a preemptive strike and attacking him."

Ong Khan, thinking these words extremely unlikely and highly displeasing, said, "Jamuqa is a blatherer, of no consequence, and untrustworthy. His words should not be listened to."

Several days then passed, and Genghis Khan became separated from them and camped farther away until the next spring of the Year of the Pig, corresponding to 599 [1203], when Sangun sent a messenger to his father, saying with all petulance, "Intelligent men who are far-sighted are saying such things. How can you not listen?"

When Ong Khan heard this insistence, he said, "It was through him that we became somebody. He has helped us many times, risking his possessions and his head. How can one think of attacking him? What can I say? The more I tell you no, the more you refuse to listen. In my old age I say let my bones rest in one place. Now that you hear, if you can do this thing, God willing you will prove capable." This he said and became very sad.

After that, they sneaked into the meadow where Genghis Khan was camped and burned it in such a way that he did not know it was they who had done it. Then they plotted, saying, "Once before, he asked for our daughter Cha'ur Beki for his son Jochi, but we did not give her. Now let us send word and say, 'We will give our daughter. Come for the banquet.' Let them give a *buljar* [ceremonial engagement meal] for us to eat. When he comes we will seize him." To this end they dispatched Bundai Qijat. (In the Naiman language and that of some other Mongols a *bökä'ül* is called *qisat*, which the Mongols call *qijat*.)

When the message was delivered, Genghis Khan set out with two liege men. Along the way he stopped to sleep at the tent of Münglig Echigä of the Qongqotan, the father of Täb Tängri. The next morning he took counsel with Münglig Echigä, who said, "Our animals are lean. Let's fatten them up. Let's send one person for the banquet but not to partake of the *buljar*."

Genghis Khan sent the messenger back and went home.

After that, Ong Khan and Sangun planned to mount an attack on Genghis Khan while he was off guard. One of Ong Khan's great commanders, Yäkä Chärän by name, went home and said to his wife, Alaq Yidun, "If somebody goes to inform Genghis Khan of what has taken place, he will reward him handsomely."

"I hope nobody hears the nonsense you say or gives it credence," his wife said.

One of Yäkä Chärän's herdsmen, Qishliq by name, had come to bring milk. Standing outside, he heard this exchange and said to his servant Badai, "Did you hear what they are saying?"

Chärän's son Narin Köhän was standing outside, filing arrows. He heard the conversation between his father and mother and said,

"May your tongues be cut out! What is this you are saying? What secrets are you divulging?"

Badai comprehended and said to Qishliq, "Now we know what's up." Immediately they went to inform Genghis Khan. (The group of *tarkhans* who are now known, Khwarazmi Tarkhan, Noqan Tarkhan, and Sadaq Tarkhan, are all descended from Qishliq and Badai. From that time until now, they and their clans have been *tarkhans* and great amirs for this reason.)

After that, when Genghis Khan understood perfectly what the words meant, he stopped in the place called Aral and ordered his tents to move toward the Silji'üljüt hills. He sent Jälmä as scout to Mau Ündür behind the mountain. Ong Khan was headed for the front side of Mount Mau Ündür, to a place where red willow trees were growing, which the Mongols call Hula'an Buruqat. Two of Alchidai Noyan's liege men, Taichu and Chigitäi Yadir, had taken the horses out in herds. They saw the enemy and immediately galloped to inform Genghis Khan, who was off guard in Qalajin. At once Genghis Khan mounted, and when the sun had risen the length of a lance, the armies of both sides drew up their ranks opposite each other. Since Genghis Khan's forces were few, while Ong Khan's were numerous, he took counsel with his commanders. "What are we to do?" he asked. One of the commanders who was there was Kähätäi Noyan of the Uru'ut, and another was Quyildar Sächän of the Mangqut, who were related to each other. (When the Uru'ut and Mangqut clans had gotten angry and left Genghis Khan to join the Tayichi'ut, these two had not rebelled and continued to perform valiantly in his service.) When Genghis Khan took counsel, Kähätäi Noyan stroked his horse's mane with his whip and sat pensive and hesitant, not giving a ready answer. Quyildar Sächän was Genghis Khan's *anda*, and he said, "Khan *anda* of mine, let me go and plant my standard behind the enemy on the hill called Köyitän and thus show my valor. If I die, I have two or three sons. Genghis Khan will take charge of caring for them and bringing them up."

—— of Mangqut lineage also said, "All this is obscuring [our real purpose]. Let us charge them, trusting in God, and see what lot God has in store for us."

In short, Quyildar galloped as he had said, and God helped him and made a way for him to pass through the foe and plant his standard on Köyitän Hill.

* * *

Genghis Khan Sends an Emissary to Ong Khan, Reminding Him of the Obligations He Owed Him

After that, Genghis Khan assigned a man named Arqai Je'ün of the Ildürgin to go to Ong Khan as emissary and deliver a message saying, "At this time I have camped in Tünggä Na'ur and Quruqa Qoroqan. The grass here is fine, and the geldings have grown fat. Now, O khan my father, aforetime your uncle Gürkhan said to you, 'You did not allow me the place of my elder brother, Buyuruq Khan, and you annihilated my two brothers Ta[i] Temür Taishi and Buqa Temür.' Therefore he chased you away, sent you into the narrows called Qara'un Qabchal, and surrounded you there. From there you emerged with several men. Who got you out if not my father who rode on military expeditions with you? A man of the Tayichi'ut named Udur Qunan and another named Buqaji went with you along with a few men, and from there [my father] went, passing through a place and a plain called Qara Buqa and crossing Qulatan Tülängütäi, headed up the *qabchal* [defile]. Gürkhan was at a place called Qurban Täläsüt. He drove [Gürkhan] out of there and put him to rout. It is not known whether he went forth with twenty men or thirty. When he went into Qashin territory he never came out again and was seen no more. My late father took the kingship from Gürkhan and gave it to you, and therefore you became *anda* with my father. I call you 'khan-father' for the same reason. Of all the favors for which you are in my debt, this is the first.

"Another time, O khan father of mine, when you had become covered and hidden beneath the clouds, and where the sun sets you were nowhere to be found, in the midst of Cha'uqut territory I called out in a loud voice to Jagambu Anda. I motioned by taking off my hat, and I did *dalaimishi*, i.e. I waved my hands. Thereby I brought Jagambu Anda, and when I brought him he sat in ambush in repayment of my enmity. Another time a troop of the Märkit tribe put

Jagambu Anda to flight. In chivalry and manliness I rescued him. Why would someone who brings Jagambu Anda from Cha'uqut territory (meaning the territory of Cathay) and saves him from the hands of the Märkit want to kill him? For your sake I killed my elder brother and destroyed my younger brother. If anyone asks who they are, they are Sacha Beki, who was my elder brother, and Taichu Qori, who was my younger brother. This is another favor you owe me.

"Another time, O khan father of mine, you came to me like the sun emerging from behind a cloud, like a fire slowly coming out. I did not leave you hungry until midday but fed you all. I did not leave you naked for a month but clothed you all. If anyone asks, 'What does he mean?' then say, 'In the place of the hill of Qati'liq, that is the place where there was arrow wood, behind the place called Mürichaq Sä'ü[l], I did battle and raided the Märkit people, seizing all their herds, flocks, tents, camps, and fine clothing and giving them to you.' As I have said, I did not let noon go by before alleviating your hunger, and I did not let a month pass before clothing your nakedness—these deeds constitute the third obligation I hold over you.

"Another time, after that, when the Märkit people were in the plain of Buqar Kähär, we sent an emissary to Toqto'a Beki to spy and gather information. When there was an opportunity you did not stop and wait for me. You galloped away before me and took captive Toqto'a Beki's and his brother's wives and Qutuqtai Khatun and [Cha'alun] Khatun. You gave me nothing. After that, when we rode against the Naiman and drew up our battle lines opposite them at Baidaraq Belchir, you captured both Qudu and Chila'un. They surrendered to you and then escaped with their soldiers and folk. Then Kögsä'ü Sabraq made a *taplamishi* [encounter], staged a raid with the Naiman army, and plundered your folk. At that time I sent Bo'orchi, Muqali, Boroghul, and Chila'un, all four, and when I had recovered your *ulus* I gave it back to you. This is the fourth favor your owe me.

"Another time, from there we came together at the Qara River, there where Hula'an Bolta'ut is, near the mountain named Jorqal Qun, and there we made a pact that if a snake with fangs and teeth brought its fangs and teeth between us, we would not part from one another until we had spoken with tongues, mouth, and teeth, that is, if anyone were to speak words of selfish interest or otherwise between us, we would not give it credence, get angry, or part ways until we had come together and investigated it. Now we have not come together to investigate and verify the words spoken to create discord between us, yet you have parted believing them and relying on them.

"Another, O khan father of mine. After that, I flew like a falcon to Mount Jurqu. I left Bu'ir Na'ur and caught cranes whose feet are bound and which are gray in color. If you ask which they were, they were the Dörbän and Tatar folk. Another time I became a gray falcon, passed through Kökä Na'ur, caught blue cranes with blue feet for you, and gave them to you. If you ask which they are, they are the Qataqin, Salji'ut, and Qunqirat people, the very ones with whose help you now threaten me. This is another of the favors for which you are indebted to me.

"Another thing, O khan father of mine. What have you done that I should be obliged to you? What profit has accrued to me from you? I hold all these obligations over you, and you have profited greatly from me. O khan father of mine, why do you threaten me? Why do you not rest in ease and comfort? Why do you not let your daughters-in-law and sons sleep in peace? I, your son, have never said that my portion is small and I want more, or that it is bad and I want better. When one of a cart's two wheels breaks it cannot travel. If an ox gets hurt, and the driver is alone and sets out having put his load on the ox, a robber will steal [the cart]. If he doesn't take the ox and leaves it with the cart, it will sicken and die. If one of a cart's two wheels is broken and the ox tries to pull it, it cannot. If it exerts itself to pull it uphill, the ox's neck will be chafed, and it will get restless, jump around, and exhaust itself. Like a cart with two wheels, I was one wheel of your cart." This was the message Genghis Khan sent to Ong Khan.

Rashid al-Din, *Compendium of Chronicles*, translated by Wheeler Thackston (Cambridge: Harvard University Department of Near Eastern Languages and Civilizations, 3 vols., 1998), 144, 174, 184, 186–88.

DISCUSSION QUESTIONS

1. Identify the similarities and differences between Rashid al-Din's and the *Secret History of the Mongols*' versions of Chinggis's relations with Jamukha and the Ong Khan.
2. Analyze Chinggis's rhetoric about his relations with the Ong Khan. Is his analysis credible?

The Secret History of the Mongols

The Secret History of the Mongols, *which was probably written during the reign of Chinggis's son Ögödei, reflects the interests of the royal family. In this selection, the author helps to legitimize Ögödei by stating that Chinggis personally chose his son as his successor.*

See the headnote on p. 43 for additional information on this text.

"The Khan will cross the high mountain passes,
cross over wide rivers,
waging a long war far from home.
Before he leaves has he thought about setting his people in order?
There is no eternity for all things born in this world.
When your body falls like an old tree
who will rule your people,
these fields of tangled grasses?
When your body crumbles like an old pillar
who will rule your people,
these great flocks of birds?
Which of your four heroic sons will you name?
What I've said everyone knows is true,
your sons, your commanders, all the common people,
even someone as low as myself.
You should decide now who it will be."
Chingis Khan replied:
"Even though she's only a woman,
what Yesui says is quite right.

My commanders, my sons, Bogorchu, Mukhali, and the others,
none of you have had the nerve to say this to me.
I've been forgetting it as if I won't follow my ancestors someday.
I've been sleeping like I won't someday be taken by death.
Jochi, you are my eldest son.
What do you say?"
But before Jochi could speak, Chagadai spoke up:
"When you tell Jochi to speak
do you offer him the succession?
How could we allow ourselves to be ruled
by this bastard son of a Merkid?"
Jochi rose up and grabbed Chagadai by the collar, saying:
"I've never been set apart from my brothers by my father the Khan.
What gives you the right to say that I'm different?
What makes you any better than I am?
Maybe your heart is harder than mine,
that's the only difference I can see.
If you can shoot an arrow farther than I can,
I'll cut off my thumb and throw it away.
If you can beat me at wrestling,
I'll lay still on the ground where I fall.
Let the word of our father the Khan decide."

* * *

The Reign of Ogodei Khan

In the Year of the Rat a Great Assembly was called.
All the people of the Right Wing
led by Chagadai and Jochi's son Batu came.
All the people of the Left Wing arrived,
led by Prince Odchigin and Khasar's sons, Yegu and Yesunge.
The people of the Middle Wing were led by Tolui,
and with him were all the royal daughters and their husbands.
This huge assembly met at Kodegu Aral on the Kerulen River,
and according to the wishes of Chingis Khan
they raised up Ogodei as the Great Khan.
Chagadai raised up his younger brother as the Khan

and both Elder Brother Chagadai and Tolui
delivered the nightguard, the archers, and the eight thousand dayguards to Ogodei,
the same men who had guarded the golden life of their father Chingis Khan,
along with his private slaves and the ten thousand men who had served him.
They also gave him command of all the people of the Middle Wing.

The Secret History of the Mongols, translated by Paul Kahn (San Francisco: North Point Press, 1984), 166–67, 182.

DISCUSSION QUESTIONS

1. What was the system of succession Chinggis devised? Why was it followed only once after his reign?
2. Why did Ögödei refer to his brothers after he was enthroned? Did the Great Khan have dictatorial powers?

Juvaini, The History of the World Conqueror

Juvaini (1226–1283), born to an elite family in Central Asia, was an official in the Il-Khanate from the beginning of its conquests in Iran and Iraq. Recruited by the Il-Khan Hülegü, who led the campaigns, he witnessed the Mongol khan's attack on the Ismaili (Order of the Assassins) center at the mountain fortress of Alamut. Before its complete destruction, Hülegü permitted Juvaini to gather and preserve the most valuable manuscripts in the Ismaili library. Once Hülegü occupied Baghdad, he appointed Juvaini as its governor. Like many Il-Khanate officials, Juvaini was affected by the intrigues that plagued and undermined Mongol rule. One of his enemies accused him and his brother, a grand vizier, of theft of government money as well as of collaboration with the Mamluks of Egypt against the Il-Khanate. Juvaini was detained for a time but was eventually released. However, he remained under suspicion until his death in 1283. His brother was not as fortunate; he and his four sons were executed in the following year.

Juvaini's History of the World Conqueror *is as important as his government responsibilities. He started on the work before Hülegü recruited him, and he recounted the Mongol campaigns through the assault on Alamut. He relied principally on eyewitnesses because most of the incidents he described occurred before his birth. Because he was an official in the Mongol administration, he was somewhat constrained in his criticisms of their invasions of Central Asia and Iran. Yet he was loyal to his native land and was appalled at the damage inflicted on his people and their territories. Such ambivalence gives his work added credibility because he records the invaders' destruction and massacres while at the same time praising the Mongols for their tolerance of many religions, their support for Islam, and their brilliant military strategy and tactics.*

And thereafter he [Chinggis] was wont to urge the strengthening of the edifice of concord and the consolidation of the foundations of affection between sons and brothers; and used continually to sow the seed of harmony and concord in the breasts of his sons and brothers and kinsfolk and to paint in their hearts the picture of mutual aid and assistance. And by means of parables he would fortify that edifice and reinforce those foundations. One day he called his sons together and taking an arrow from his quiver he broke it in half. Then he took two arrows and broke them also. And he continued to add to the bundle until there were so many arrows that even athletes were unable to break them. Then turning to his sons he said: 'So it is with you also. A frail arrow, when it is multiplied and supported by its fellows, not even mighty warriors are able to break it but in impotence withdraw their hands therefrom. As long, therefore, as you brothers support one another and render stout assistance one to another, though your enemies be men of great strength and might, yet shall they not gain the victory over you.

* * *

When the party arrived at Otrar, the governor of that town was one Inalchuq, who was a kinsman of the Sultan's mother, Terken Khatun, and had received the title of Ghayir-Khan. Now amongst the merchants was an Indian who had been acquainted with the governor in former times. He now addressed the latter simply as Inalchuq; and being rendered proud by reason of the power and might of his own Khan he did not stand aloof from him nor have regard to his own interests. On this account Ghayir-Khan became annoyed and embarrassed; at the same time he conceived a desire for their property. He therefore placed them under arrest, and sent a messenger to the Sultan in Iraq to inform him about them. Without pausing to think the Sultan sanctioned the shedding of their blood and deemed the seizure of their goods to be lawful, not knowing that his own life would become unlawful, nay a crime, and that the bird of his prosperity would be lopped of feather and wing.

> He whose soul hath understanding looketh to the capital
> of deeds.

Ghayir-Khan in executing his command deprived these men of their lives and possessions, nay rather he desolated and laid waste a whole world and rendered a whole creation without home, property or leaders. For every drop of their blood there flowed a whole Oxus; in retribution for every hair on their heads it seemed that a hundred thousand heads rolled in the dust at every crossroad; and in exchange for every dinar a thousand *qintars* were exacted.

> Our property was plunder, and our hopes in vain; our affairs in a state of anarchy, and our counsels but the advice of one another.
> And they drove away our beasts of burden and led off our chargers beneath loads that crushed their saddles,
> Loads of furniture, clothing, money and goods; what had been acquired by purchase and stored up in treasuries.
> To this hath Fate condemned some of her people; the calamities of some appear a feast to others.

Before this order arrived one of the merchants devised a stratagem and escaped from the straits of prison. Having acquainted himself with the state of affairs and ascertained the position of his friends, he set his face to the road, made his way to the Khan and informed him of what had befallen his companions. These tidings had such an effect upon the Khan's mind that the control of repose and tranquillity was removed, and the whirlwind of anger cast dust into the eyes of patience and clemency while the fire of wrath flared up with such a flame that it drove the water from his eyes and could be quenched only by the shedding of blood. In this fever Chingiz-Khan went up alone to the summit of a hill, bared his head, turned his face towards the earth and for three days and nights offered up prayer, saying: 'I was not the author of this trouble; grant me strength to exact vengeance.' Thereupon he descended from the hill, meditating action and making ready for war. And since Küchlüg and Toq-Toghan, the fugitives from his army, lay across his path, he first sent an army to deal with their mischief and sedition, as has been previously mentioned. He then dispatched envoys to the Sultan to remind him of the treachery which he had needlessly occasioned and to advise him of his intention to march against him; so that he might prepare for war and equip himself with thrusting and striking weapons.

Now it is a fully established fact that whoever sows a dry root never reaps any harvest therefrom, while whoever plants the sapling of opposition by common consent gathers the fruit thereof, namely repentance and regret. And so the beatified Sultan because of the harshness of his disposition and the violence of his custom and nature was involved in grave danger; and in the end his posterity had to taste the bile of punishment therefor and his successors to suffer the bitterness of adversity.

> If thou doest evil, thou dost punish thyself; the eye
> of Fate is not asleep.
> Bizhan's picture is still painted on the walls of palaces;
> he is in the prison of Afrasiyab.

* * *

Of the Capture of Bokhara

In the Eastern countries it is the cupola of Islam and is in those regions like unto the City of Peace [Baghdad]. Its environs are adorned with the brightness of the light of doctors and jurists and its surroundings embellished with the rarest of high attainments. Since ancient times it has in every age been the place of assembly of the great savants of every religion. Now the derivation of Bokhara is from *bukhar*, which in the language of the Magians signifies *centre of learning*. This word closely resembles a word in the language of the Uighur and Khitayan idolaters, who call their places of worship, which are idol-temples, *bukhar.* But at the time of its foundation the name of the town was Bumijkath.

Chingiz-Khan, having completed the organization and equipment of his armies, arrived in the countries of the Sultan; and dispatching his elder sons and the *noyans* in every direction at the head of large forces, he himself advanced first upon Bokhara, being accompanied by Toli alone of his elder sons and by a host of fearless Turks that knew not clean from unclean, and considered the bowl of war to be a basin of rich soup and held a mouthful of the sword to be a beaker of wine.

He proceeded along the road to Zarnuq, and in the morning when the king of the planets raised his banner on the eastern horizon, he arrived unexpectedly before the town. When the inhabitants thereof, who were unaware of the fraudulent designs of Destiny, beheld the surrounding countryside choked with horsemen and the air black as night with the dust of cavalry, fright and panic overcame them, and fear and dread prevailed. They betook themselves to the citadel and closed the gates, thinking, 'This is perhaps a single detachment of a great army and a single wave from a raging sea.' It was their intention to resist and to approach calamity on their own feet, but they were aided by divine grace so that they stood firm and breathed not opposition. At this juncture, the World-Emperor, in accordance with his constant practice, dispatched Danishmand Hajib upon an embassy to them, to announce the arrival of his forces and to advise them to stand out of the way of a dreadful deluge. Some of the inhabitants, who were in the category of '*Satan hath gotten mastery over them*', were minded to do him harm and mischief; whereupon he raised a shout, saying: 'I am such-and-such a person, a Moslem and the son of a Moslem. Seeking God's pleasure I am come on an embassy to you, at the inflexible command of Chingiz-Khan, to draw you out of the whirpool of destruction and the trough of blood. It is Chingiz-Khan himself who has come with many thousands of warriors. The battle has reached thus far. If you are incited to resist in any way, in an hour's time your citadel will be level ground and the plain a sea of blood. But if you will listen to advice and exhortation with the ear of intelligence and consideration and become submissive and obedient to his command, your lives and property will remain in the stronghold of security.' When the people, both nobles and commoners, had heard his words, which bore the brand of veracity, they did not refuse to accept his advice, knowing for certain that the flood might not be stemmed by their obstructing his passage nor might the quaking of the mountains and the earth be quietened and allayed by the pressure of their feet. And so they held it proper to choose peace and advantageous to accept advice. But by way of caution and security they obtained from him a covenant that if, after the people had gone forth to meet the Khan and obeyed his command, any harm should befall any one of them, the retribution thereof should be on his head. Thus were the people's minds set at ease, and they withdrew their feet from the thought of transgression and turned their faces towards the path of advantage. The chief men of Zarnuq sent forward a delegation bearing presents. When these came to the place where the Emperor's cavalry had halted, he asked about their leaders and notables and was wroth with them for their dilatoriness in remaining behind. He dispatched a messenger to summon them to his presence. Because of the great awe in which the Emperor was held a tremor of horror appeared on the limbs of these people like the quaking of the members of a mountain. They at once proceeded to his presence; and when they arrived he treated them with mercy and clemency and spared their lives, so that they were once more of good heart.

* * *

And his troops were more numerous than ants or locusts, being in their multitude beyond estimation or computation. Detachment after detachment arrived, each like a billowing sea, and encamped round about the town. At sunrise twenty thousand men from the Sultan's auxiliary *(bīrūnī)* army issued forth from the citadel together with most of the inhabitants; being commanded by Kök-Khan and other officers such as Khamid-Bur, Sevinch-Khan and Keshli-Khan. Kök-Khan was said to be a Mongol and to have fled from Chingiz-Khan and joined the Sultan *(the proof of which statements must rest with their author);* as a consequence of which his affairs had greatly prospered. When these forces reached the banks of the Oxus, the patrols and advance parties of the Mongol army fell upon them and left no trace of them.

When it is impossible to flee from destruction in any
manner, then patience is the best and wisest course.

On the following day when from the reflection of the sun the plain seemed to be a tray filled with blood, the people of Bokhara opened their gates and closed the door of strife and battle. The *imams* and notables came on a deputation to Chingiz-Khan, who entered to inspect the town and the citadel. He rode into the Friday mosque and pulled up before the *maqsura,* whereupon his son Toli dismounted and ascended the pulpit. Chingiz-Khan asked those present whether this was the palace of the Sultan; they replied that it was the house of God. Then he too got down from his horse, and mounting two or three steps of the pulpit he exclaimed: 'The countryside is empty of fodder; fill our horses' bellies.' Whereupon they opened all the magazines in the town and began carrying off the grain. And they brought the cases in which the Korans were kept out into the courtyard of the mosque, where they cast the Korans right and left and turned the cases into mangers for their horses. After which they circulated cups of wine and sent for the singing-girls of the town to sing and dance for them; while the Mongols raised their voices to the tunes of their own songs. Meanwhile, the *imams, shaikhs, sayyids,* doctors and scholars of the age kept watch over their horses in the stable under the supervision of the equerries, and executed their commands. After an hour or two Chingiz-Khan arose to return to his camp, and as the multitude that had been gathered there moved away the leaves of the Koran were trampled in the dirt beneath their own feet and their horses' hoofs. In that moment, the Emir Imam Jalal-ad-Din 'Ali b. al-Hasan Zaidi, who was the chief and leader of the *sayyids* of Transoxiana and was famous for his piety and asceticism, turned to the learned *imam* Rukn-ad-Din Imamzada, who was one of the most excellent savants in the world—*may God render pleasant the resting-places of them both*—and said: '*Maulana,* what state is this?

That which I see do I see it in wakefulness or in sleep, O Lord?'

Maulana Imamzada answered: 'Be silent: it is the wind of God's omnipotence that bloweth, and we have no power to speak.'

When Chingiz-Khan left the town he went to the festival *musalla* and mounted the pulpit; and, the people having been assembled, he asked which were the wealthy amongst them. Two hundred and eighty persons were designated (a hundred and ninety of them being natives of the town and the rest strangers, viz. ninety merchants from various places and were led before him. He then began a speech, in which, after describing the resistance and treachery of the Sultan (of which more than enough has been said already) he addressed them as follows: 'O people, know that you have committed great sins, and that the great ones among you have committed these sins. If you ask me what proof I have for these words, I say it is because I am the punishment of God. If you had not committed great sins, God would not have sent a punishment like me upon you.' When he had finished speaking in this strain, he continued his discourse with words of admonition, saying, 'There is no need to declare your property that is on the face of the earth; tell me of that which is in the belly of the earth.' Then he asked them who were their men of authority; and each man indicated his own people. To each of them he assigned a Mongol or Turk as *basqaq* in order that the soldiers might not molest them, and, although not subjecting them to disgrace or humiliation, they began to exact money from these men; and when they delivered it up they did not torment them by excessive punishment or demanding what was beyond their power to pay. And every day, at the rising of the greater luminary, the guards would bring a party of notables to the audience-hall of the World-Emperor.

Chingiz-Khan had given orders for the Sultan's troops to be driven out of the interior of the town and the citadel. As it was impossible to accomplish this purpose by employing the townspeople and as these troops, being in fear of their lives, were fighting, and doing battle, and making night attacks as much as was possible, he now gave orders for all the quarters of the town to be set on fire; and since the houses were built entirely of wood, within several days the greater part of the town had been consumed, with the exception of the Friday mosque and some of the palaces, which were built with baked bricks. Then the people of Bokhara were driven against the citadel. And on either side the furnace of battle was heated. On the outside, mangonels were erected, bows bent and stones and arrows discharged; and on the inside, ballistas and pots of naphtha were set in motion. It was like a red-hot furnace fed from without by hard sticks thrust into the recesses, while from the belly of the furnace sparks shoot into the air. For days they fought in this manner; the garrison made sallies against the besiegers, and Kök-Khan in particular, who in bravery would have borne the palm from male lions, engaged in many battles: in each attack he overthrew several persons and alone repelled a great army. But finally they were reduced to the last extremity; resistance was no longer in their power; and they stood excused before God and man. The moat had been filled with animate and inanimate and raised up with levies and Bokharians; the outworks *(fasil)* had been captured and fire hurled into the citadel; and their khans, leaders and notables, who were the chief men of the age and the favourites of the Sultan and who in their glory would set their feet on the head of Heaven, now became the captives of abasement and were drowned in the sea of annihilation.

> Fate playeth with mankind the game of the sticks with the ball,
> Or the game of the wind blowing (know thou!) a handful of millet.
> Fate is a hunter, and man is naught but a lark.

Of the Qanqli no male was spared who stood higher than the butt of a whip and more than thirty thousand were counted amongst the slain; whilst their small children, the children of their nobles and their womenfolk, slender as the cypress, were reduced to slavery.

When the town and the citadel had been purged of rebels and the walls and outworks levelled with the dust, all the inhabitants of the town, men and women, ugly and beautiful, were driven out on to the field of the *musalla*. Chingiz-Khan spared their lives; but the youths and full-grown men that were fit for such service were pressed into a levy *(hasbar)* for the attack on Samarqand and Dabusiya. Chingiz-Khan then proceeded against Samarqand; and the people of Bokhara, because of the desolation, were scattered like the constellation of the Bear and departed into the villages, while the site of the town became like *'a level plain.'*

Now one man had escaped from Bokhara after its capture and had come to Khorasan. He was questioned about the fate of that city and replied: 'They came, they sapped, they burnt, they slew, they plundered and they departed.' Men of understanding who heard this description were all agreed that in the Persian language there could be nothing more concise than this speech. And indeed all that has been written in this chapter is summed up and epitomized in these two or three words.

***

When Chingiz-Khan arrived at Otrar the news had been spread abroad of the strengthening of the walls and the citadel of Samarqand and the great size of its garrison; and everyone was of the opinion that it would be a matter of years before the town could be taken, to say nothing of the citadel. Following the path of circumspection he held it expedient to purge the surrounding country before proceeding against the town. First of all, he advanced against Bokhara, and when his mind had been set at rest by the capture of that city, he concerned himself with the question of Samarqand. Turning his reins in that direction he drove before him a great levy raised in Bokhara; and whenever the villages on his path submitted, he in no way molested them; but wherever they offered resistance, as in Sari-Pul and Dabusiya, he left troops to besiege them, while he himself made no halt until he reached Samarqand. When his sons had disposed of the affair of Otrar, they too arrived with a levy raised in that town; they chose the Kök-Sarai for Chingiz-Khan's encampment. The other troops also, as they arrived, encamped round about the town.

For a day or two Chingiz-Khan circled the town in person in order to inspect the walls, the outworks and the gates; and during this period he exempted his men from fighting. At the same time he dispatched Yeme and Sübetei, who were two of the great *noyans* and enjoyed his special trust, in pursuit of the Sultan together with thirty thousand men; and sent Ghadaq Noyan and Yasa'ur to Vakhsh and Talaqan.

Finally, on the third day, when the flare of the sun's flame had risen from the darkness of the pitchy night's smoke and the nocturnal blackness had retired to the seclusion of a corner, so many men, both Mongols and levies, were assembled together that their numbers exceeded those of the sand of the desert or drops of rain. They stationed themselves in a circle round about the town; and Alp-Er Khan, Shaikh Khan, Bala Khan and some other khans made a sally into the open, drew up opposite the army of the world-subduing Emperor and discharged their arrows. Many horse and foot were slain on either side. That day the Sultan's Turks engaged in constant skirmishes with the Mongols—for the light of the candle flares up a little before going out—killing some of the Mongol army, capturing others and carrying them into the town, while a thousand of their own number likewise fell.

Finally,

> When for the benefit of the earth the fire of heaven
> was hidden by the earth's smoke,

everyone retired to his quarters. But as soon as the deceitful shield-bearer again struck his sword upon the cloud of night, Chingiz-Khan mounted in person and stationed his troops in a circle round about the town. Both inside and outside the troops assembled and made ready for battle; and they pulled up the girth of combat and hostility until the time of evening prayer. From the discharge of mangonels and bows, arrows and stones were set in flight; and the Mongol army took up a position at the very gates and so prevented the Sultan's troops from issuing forth on to the field of battle. And when the path of combat was closed to them, and the two parties had become entangled on the chess-board of war and the valiant knights were no longer able to manoeuvre their horses upon the plain, they threw in their elephants; but the Mongols did not turn tail, on the contrary with their King-checking arrows they liberated those that were held in check by the elephants and broke up the ranks of the infantry. When the elephants had received wounds and were of no more use than the foot-soldiers of chess, they turned back trampling many people underneath their feet. At length, when the Emperor of Khotan [the Sun] had let down the veil over his face, they closed the gates.

The people of Samarqand had been rendered apprehensive by this day's fighting, and their passions and opinions were divergent: some were desirous of submission and surrender, while others feared for their lives; some, by heavenly decree, were restrained from making peace, while others, because of the aura diffused by Chingiz-Khan, were prevented from doing battle. Finally, on the next day

When the shining sun spread its glory, and the black
raven of the firmament shed its feathers,

the Mongol troops being bold and fearless and the people of Samarqand irresolute in mind and counsel, the latter put the idea of war out of their heads and ceased to resist. The cadi and the *shaikh-al-Islam* together with a number of wearers of the turban hastened to approach Chingiz-Khan: they were fortified and encouraged by the breakfast of his promises and with his permission re-entered the town.

At the time of prayer they opened the gate of the *musalla* and closed the door of resistance. The Mongols then entered and that day busied themselves with the destruction of the town and its outworks. The inhabitants drew their feet beneath the skirt of security, and the Mongols in no way molested them. When the day had clad itself in the black garb of the heathen Khitayans, they lit torches and continued their work until the walls had been levelled with the streets and there was everywhere free passage for horse and foot.

On the third day, when the unkind, black-hearted juggler of the blue countenance held up the hard, brazen mirror before his face, the greater part of the Mongols entered the town, and the men and women in groups of a hundred were driven out into the open in the charge of Mongol soldiers; only the cadi and the *shaikh-al-Islam* together with such as had some connection with them and stood under their protection were exempted from leaving the town. More than fifty thousand people were counted who remained under such protection. The Mongols then caused a proclamation to be made that if anyone sought safety in the corner of concealment his blood should be forfeit. The Mongols and the [other] troops busied themselves with pillaging; and many people who had hidden in cellars and cavities were [discovered and] slain.

The mahouts brought their elephants to Chingiz-Khan and demanded elephant fodder. He asked them what the elephants lived on before they fell into captivity. They replied: 'The grass of the plains.' Whereupon he ordered the elephants to be set free to forage for themselves. They were accordingly released and finally perished [of hunger].

When the king of the heavens had sunk beneath the ball of the earth, the Mongols departed from the town, and the garrison of the citadel, their hearts cut in two with fear and terror, could neither stand and resist nor turn and flee. Alp Khan, however, made a show of valour and intrepidity: issuing forth from the citadel with a thousand desperate men he fought his way through the centre of the Mongol army and joined up with the Sultan. The next morning, when the heralds of the Lord of the planets rose up striking their swords, the Mongol army completely encircled the citadel, and discharging arrows and projectiles from either side they devastated the walls and outworks and laid waste the Juy-i-Arziz. During the space between the two prayers they took the gates and entered the citadel. A thousand brave and valiant men withdrew to the cathedral mosque and commenced a fierce battle using both naphtha and quarrels. The army of Chingiz-Khan likewise employed pots of naphtha; and the Friday mosque and all that were in it were burnt with the fire of this world and washed with the water of the Hereafter. Then all in the citadel were brought out into the open, where the Turks were separated from the Taziks and all divided into groups of ten and a hundred. They shaved the front of the Turks' heads in the Mongol fashion in order to tranquillize them and allay their fears; but when the sun had reached the west, the day of their life drew to its close, and that night every male Qanqli was drowned in the ocean of destruction and consumed by the fire of perdition. There were more than thirty thousand Qanqli and Turks, commanded by Barishmas[1] Khan, Taghai[2] Khan, Sarsigh[3] Khan and Ulagh[4] Khan, together with some twenty of the Sultan's chief emirs, whose names are recorded in the *yarligh* which Chingiz-Khan wrote to Rukn-ad-Din Kart; in which *yarligh* full mention is made of all the leaders of armies and countries whom he crushed and destroyed.

When the town and the citadel equalled each other in ruin and desolation and many an emir, and soldier, and townsman had

[1] *Barishmas* in Turkish means 'he that does not make peace.'

[2] *Taghai,* i.e. 'maternal uncle.'

[3] *Sarsigh* means 'hard,' 'rough.'

[4] *Ulagh* means 'post horse.'

taken a sip at the cup of destruction, on the next day, when the eagle which is the heavenly Jamshid had raised its head above the mountain-tops of the earth and the fiery countenance of the sun was lit up upon the round tray of the sky, the people who had escaped from beneath the sword were numbered; thirty thousand of them were chosen for their craftmanship, and these Chingiz-Khan distributed amongst his sons and kinsmen, while the like number were selected from the youthful and valiant to form a levy. With regard to the remainder, who obtained permission to return into the town, as a thanksgiving because they had not shared the fate of the others nor attained the degree of martyrdom but had remained in the ranks of the living, he imposed [a ransom of] two hundred thousand dinars on these suppliants and deputed the collection of this sum to Siqat-al-Mulk and 'Amid Buzurg, who belonged to the chief officials of Samarqand. He then appointed several persons to be *shahnas* of the town and took some of the levies with him to Khorasan, while the others he sent to Khorazm with his sons. And afterwards, several times in succession levies were raised in Samarqand and few only were exempted therefrom; and for this reason complete ruin overran the country.

Juvaini, *The History of the World Conqueror*, translated by John Boyle (Manchester: Manchester University Press, 2 vols., 1958), 41, 79–81, 97–100, 103–07, 117–22.

DISCUSSION QUESTIONS

1. Why was Chinggis so determined to emphasize unity? What is the difference between a tribe and a confederation?
2. What was the Mongol attitude toward envoys and their safe passage?
3. How did Chinggis prompt voluntary submission?
4. According to Juvaini, what did Chinggis want in his Central Asian campaigns?
5. According to Juvaini, "no male was spared who stood higher than the butt of a whip." How did such reports assist the Mongols in their campaigns?
6. What did the Mongol campaigns against Bukhara and Samarkand reveal about their increased sophistication in warfare?

7. Why did Chinggis spare thirty thousand craftsmen in Samarkand?
8. The Mongols traditionally relied on cavalry in warfare. What tactics and strategy were more critical in Central Asia?

The Travels of Ibn Battuta

Like Marco Polo and Rabban Sauma, Ibn Battuta (1304–1368/69) spanned two continents in his travels. Unlike the other two voyagers, he journeyed to Asia and Africa, not Asia and Europe. His initial travels mirrored those of Rabban Sauma because he too started on a religious pilgrimage. Trained in the law in his native city of Tangier, he set forth in 1325 on a hajj *to the city of Mecca. During this voyage, he also visited other sites in North Africa and the Middle East. His delightful experiences on this journey prompted a thirty-year career of travels, which led him to the Byzantine empire, India, Central Asia, Afghanistan, Tanzania, Mali, Sri Lanka, Myanmar, Grenada, and perhaps China. Traveling principally in the Islamic world, he earned his living, in part, as a* qadi *or judge. The relative ease of his travels, with a notable lack of banditry or other impediments along the Silk Roads, attests to the* Pax Mongolica's *impact on the flow of people, products, ideas, and technologies across Eurasia. On his return to his homeland in the mid-1350s, the sultan of Morocco commanded Ibn Juzayy to write the* Rihla, *which documented Ibn Battuta's travels and observations. Like Marco Polo's and Rabban Sauma's accounts, errors and inconsistencies in the work may be due to their amanuensis's misunderstandings.*

Ibn Battuta's descriptions of the Islamic world are more accurate than his accounts of the non-Islamic populations. His portraits of Sufi thinkers, mosques, education, Mecca, Muslim merchants' trade via the Persian Gulf, and vibrant cities tally with historical records. However, his depiction of China is vague and imprecise, prompting questions about whether he actually reached East Asia. Because he dealt mostly with the elites, he scarcely comments on the lives and customs of ordinary people. Nonetheless, his text yields considerable information about the conduct of official affairs as well as banquets and ceremonies in various Islamic states. His visit to the Golden Horde's Khan Özbeg, who had converted to Islam, is particularly instructive. He reveals that the capital at

Sarai had at least twelve mosques, indicating a growing Turkic and Mongol attraction to Islam. He is also impressed with the power of the khatuns, *the khan's wives, an observation that conforms with other accounts of elite Mongol women. He may have obtained the information in this selection during his stay with the Golden Horde.*

Narrative of the Origin of the Tatars and of Their Devastation of Bukhārā and Other Cities

Tankiz Khan was a blacksmith in the land of al-Khata, and he was a man of generous soul, and strength, and well-developed body. He used to assemble the people and supply them with food. After a while a company [of warriors] gathered around him and appointed him as their commander. He gained the mastery in his own country, grew in strength and power of attack and became a formidable figure. He subdued the king of al-Khata and then the king of China, his armies became immense in size, and he conquered the lands of al-Khutan, Kashkhar, and Almaliq.[1] Jalal al-Din Sanjar, son of Khwarizm Shah, the king of Khwarizm, Khurasan, and Transoxiana, [however], possessed great power and military strength, so Tankiz stood in awe of him, kept out of his [territories], and avoided any conflict with him.

It happened that Tankiz sent a party of merchants with the wares of China and al-Khata, such as silk fabrics etc., to the town of Utrar, which was the last place in the government of Jalal al-Din. His governor in the town sent a message to him, informing him of this event, and enquiring of him what action he should take in regard to them. Jalal al-Din wrote to him, commanding him to seize their goods, mutilate them, cut off their limbs and send them back to their country—[displaying thereby], because of what God Most High willed to inflict of distress and suffering for their faith upon

[1] Khata or Khitay ('Cathay') was the name given to the northern and northwestern provinces of China, which constituted a separate kingdom under the Khitan or Liao dynasty (see E. Bretschneider, *Mediaeval Researches from Eastern Asiatic Sources*, London, 1910, I, 208–9). Pekin, the capital of the Chin dynasty in China proper, was captured in 1215. Kashghar and Khotan (both in Sinkiang) and Almaligh (in Semiryechye) were occupied in 1218.

the peoples of the Eastern lands, weak judgement and a bad and ill-omened management of affairs. So, when he carried out this action, Tankiz made ready to set out in person with an army of uncountable numbers to invade the lands of Islām. When the governor of Utrar heard of his advance he sent spies to bring back a report about him, and the story goes that one of them went into the *mahalla* of one of the amīrs of Tankiz, disguised as a beggar. He found nobody to give him food, and took up a position beside one of their men, but he neither saw any provisions with him nor did the man give him anything to eat. In the evening the man brought out some dry intestines that he had with him, moistened them with water, opened a vein of his horse, filled the intestines with its blood, tied them up and cooked them on a fire; this was his food. So the spy returned to Utrar, reported on them to the governor, and told him that no one had the power to fight against them. The governor then asked his king, Jalal al-Din, for reinforcements, and the latter sent him a force of sixty thousand men, over and above the troops who were already with him. When the battle was joined, Tankiz defeated them, forced his way into the city of Utrar by the sword, killed the men, and enslaved the children. Jalal al-Din [then] came out in person to engage him, and there took place between them battles such as were never known in the history of Islām.

The final result of the matter was that Tankiz gained possession of Transoxiana, laid waste Bukhara, Samarqand and Tirmidh, crossed the River [i.e. the river of Jaihun] to the city of Balkh and captured it, then [advanced] to al-Bamiyan, conquered it, and penetrated far into the lands of Khurāsān and 'Irāq al-'Ajam. The Muslims in Balkh and Transoxiana then revolted against him, so he turned back to deal with them, entered Balkh by the sword and left it 'fallen down upon its roofs'. He went on to do the same at Tirmidh; it was laid waste and never afterwards repopulated, but a [new] city was built two miles distant from it, which is nowadays called Tirmidh. He slew the population of al-Bamiyan and destroyed it completely, except for the minaret of its mosque. He pardoned the inhabitants of Bukhara and Samarqand, and returned thereafter to al-'Iraq. The advance of the Tatars continued to the point that finally they entered Baghdad, the capital of Islām and seat of the

Caliphate, by the sword and slaughtered the Caliph al-Musta'sim billāh, the 'Abbasid (God's mercy on him).

Ibn Battuta, *The Travels of Ibn Battuta,* translated by H. A. R. Gibb (Cambridge: The Hakluyt Society, 3 vols., 1958–71), 551–53.

DISCUSSION QUESTION

1. What does Ibn Battuta's account, written a century later, reveal about the knowledge and lasting legacy of Chinggis and the Mongols?

Rashid al-Din, Compendium of Chronicles

Rashid al-Din and other Persian historians describe, in great detail, the damage and massacres wrought by the Mongols. Some of these descriptions appear to be exaggerated. This selection narrates the reputed razing of Samarkand, one of the most renowned cities in Central Asia, which is currently located in the country of Uzbekistan.

See the headnote on p. 59 for additional information on this text.

Genghis Khan Heads for Samarkand and Takes It with His World-conquering Army

At the end of spring in the Moghai Yil mentioned above, which began in Dhu'l-Hijja 617 [January 1221] but most of which was in 618, Genghis Khan set out for Samarkand. Sultan Muhammad Khwarazmshah had entrusted Samarkand to 110,000 men, 60,000 of whom were Turks, with sixty demon-shaped elephants. There was such a huge throng of common people and elite alike that they could not be numbered. In addition he had fortified the walls of the fortress and constructed several outer walls around the perimeter and connected the moat to water.

When Genghis Khan arrived in Otrar he heard reports of the enormity of the army in Samarkand and the strength of its fortress and citadel, and all were agreed that it would take years to reduce the city itself to capitulation, not to mention the citadel. As a precaution he thought it best to clear the surrounding areas first, and to that end he set out for Bukhara, took it, and then drove an enormous levy to Samarkand.

* * *

When he reached Samarkand, the princes and officers who had been sent to Otrar and other territories had completed their conquests. They and the levies that had been sent there came, Kök Saray was chosen as a place for the court, and as the various contingents arrived they camped encircling the city.

Genghis Khan himself rode around the ramparts and outer walls for a day or two, contemplating tactics for taking them. During that time news arrived that the Khwarazmshah was in his summer place. Jäbä Bahadur and Sübätäi Bahadur, both great generals, were dispatched with thirty thousand men, and Alaq Noyan and Yisa'u[r] were sent to Wakhsh and Taligan.

After that, at dawn of the third day, more Mongol soldiers and levies than could be numbered encircled the city walls. The next day Alpär Khan, S[hay]kh Khan, Balan Khan, and a host of khans did battle outside, and many were killed on both sides. That night all returned to their bases. The next day Genghis Khan himself mounted, stationed all the soldiers around the perimeter of the city, and with arrow and blade forced the city fighters into the plain and battlefield. The citizens, scared by the battle that day, divided into factions.

The next day the Mongols, itching to fight, and the citizens, hesitant, began the battle again. Suddenly the cadi and the shaykhu'l-islam came to Genghis Khan with a group of people and then went back into the city, having been given promises. The next morning at prayer time they opened the gates to let the soldiers in. That day the Mongols got to work destroying the ramparts and outer fortifications, leveling them to the ground. The men and women were driven out into the plain by the hundreds, accompanied by Mongols, but the cadi and shaykhu'l-islam and their dependents were exempted from the exodus. Nearly fifty thousand men remained safe under their protection. It was heralded that anyone who hid would be killed, and as the Mongols were busy looting they killed many they found hidden in nooks and crannies. The elephant drivers took their elephants before Genghis Khan and asked for fodder for them. He ordered them turned loose in the plains to forage for themselves. The elephants were turned loose, but they perished of hunger.

That night the Mongols came out of the city, and the defenders of the fortress were in great fear. Alp[är] Khan and a thousand warriors ready to die attacked the army, emerged from the fortress, and took flight. The next morning the soldiers again stood encircling the citadel, and arrows and stones were sent flying from both sides. The ramparts and outer works of the fortress were destroyed, and the water canal was also ruined. By evening they had taken the gates and gotten inside. A thousand warriors and champions took refuge in the mosque, from inside which they fought hard with arrows and naphtha. The Mongols also hurled naphtha, took the mosque and everyone in it, and burned the lot. They drove the people of the citadel out into the plain, separating the Turks from the Tajiks, and dividing them into groups of hundreds and tens. For the Turks they made *nughula* [side locks] and forelocks, and they put the rest to death—all Qanqlis, more than thirty thousand under the command of Barishmas Khan, Taghayi Khan, Sarsigh Khan, Ulagh Khan, and some twenty-odd of the sultan's other commanders whose names Genghis Khan wrote in detail to Ruknuddin Kurt.

When the city and fortress alike lay in ruins, and many officers and soldiers had been executed, the next day those who were left were counted. Of the total, thirty thousand registered as craftsmen were distributed among the officers, commanders, and ladies. An equal number was assigned to the levy. The remainder were given permission to depart, and as a token of appreciation for their safety they were levied an amount of 200,000 dinars, which Siqatulmulk and Amir Amid Buzurg, two high-office-holding dignitaries of Samarkand, were ordered to collect. He assigned a *shahna* and took some of the levy with himself to Khurasan and sent others to his sons in Khwarazm. Several other times after that they requested levies, and few persons escaped from those levies because that region was totally devastated.

Genghis Khan spent that summer and autumn in the vicinity of Samarkand.

Rashid al-Din, *Compendium of Chronicles*, translated by Wheeler Thackston (Cambridge: Harvard University Department of Near Eastern Languages and Civilizations, 3 vols., 1998), 247–49.

DISCUSSION QUESTIONS

1. Describe the styles of the historians Juvaini and Rashid al-Din (see p. 70). Which author gives a sense of the immediacy of Chinggis's Central Asian campaigns?
2. How did Mongol policies toward enemies who submitted and those who hid facilitate future campaigns?

Changchun, The Travels of an Alchemist

Changchun (1148–1227), a leader of the Quanzhen sect of Daoism, pursued a monastic life and would have been known mostly for his religious vocation had fate, in the form of Chinggis Khan, not intruded. Becoming a Daoist monk at the age of eighteen, he led a peripatetic life, moving from one monastery to another. He became famous for his advocacy and embodiment of Quanzhen Daoism and even had an audience with Emperor Shizong of the Jin dynasty, which controlled North China from 1127 to 1234. Quanzhen was an ascetic sect that prescribed abstention from sensual pleasures and lust. Adherents were advised to avoid excessive desire, to eat simple and not overly tasty food, and to seek purity and quiet. Several adherents also counseled sleeplessness as a means of self-denial.

Chinggis's relationship with this apostle of abstemiousness seems, at first, puzzling. The Mongol khan was interested in the Daoist sect's experiments with alchemy as a means to prolong life. Changchun disclaimed any formulas for longevity, but he sufficiently impressed the Mongol ruler that Chinggis wanted to have the Daoist master accompany him on his Central Asian expedition. Even when Changchun, perhaps indiscreetly, advised the khan to sleep alone for a month to purify himself, Chinggis was not taken aback.

Changchun's disciple Li Zhichang (1193–1278) escorted him on his travels with the Mongols and wrote Xiyuji, *a primary source on the Mongol khan, about his journeys.*

It was now the twenty-ninth of the third month (May 11th) and the Master made a poem. After four more days of travelling we reached the Khan's camp. He sent his high officer, Ho-la-po-te to meet us. This was on the fifth day of the fourth month. When arrangements had been made for the Master's lodging, he at once presented himself to the Emperor, who expressed his gratitude, saying: "Other rulers summoned you, but you would not go to them. And now you have come ten thousand *li* to see me. I take this as a high compliment."

The Master replied: "That I, a hermit of the mountains, should come at your Majesty's bidding was the will of Heaven." Chingiz was delighted, begged him to be seated and ordered food to be served. Then he asked him: "Adept, what Medicine of Long Life have you brought me from afar?" The Master replied: "I have means of protecting life, but no elixir that will prolong it." The Emperor was pleased with his candour, and had two tents for the Master and his disciples set up to the east of his own.

* * *

At this season a fine rain begins to fall and the grass becomes green again. Then, after the middle of the eleventh month, the rain becomes heavier, sometimes turning to snow, and the ground becomes saturated. From the time of the Master's first arrival in Samarkand it was his habit to give what grain we could spare to the poor and hungry of the city. Often, too, he would send hot rice-meal, and in this way saved a great number of lives.

An Alchemist

On the twenty-sixth (December 30th) we set out. On the twenty-third of the twelfth month (January 26th, 1223) there was a snowstorm and such intense cold that many oxen and horses were frozen to death on the road. After three days we crossed the Khojandmürän [the Syr Darya] from west to east and soon reached the Khan's camp. Here we learnt that on the twenty-eighth, in the middle of night, the bridge of boats had broken loose and been swept away. The Khan asked the reason of calamities such as earthquakes, thunder and so on. The Master replied: "I have heard that in order to avoid the wrath of Heaven you forbid your countrymen to bathe in rivers during the summer, wash their clothes, make fresh felt or gather mushrooms in the fields. But this is not the way to serve Heaven. It is said that of the three thousand sins the worst is ill-treatment of one's father and mother. Now in this respect I believe your subjects to be gravely at fault and it would be well if your Majesty would use your influence to reform them."

This pleased the Khan and he said: "Holy Immortal, your words are exceedingly true; such is indeed my own belief," and he bade those who were present write them down in Uighur characters. The Master asked that what he had said might be made known to the Khan's subjects in general, and this was agreed to.

The Khan also summoned his sons and the other princes, high ministers and officers, and said to them: "The Chinese reverence this holy Immortal just as you revere Heaven; and I am more than ever convinced that he is indeed a Being from Heaven!" And he proceeded to repeat to them all that the Master had taught him on various occasions, adding: "Heaven sent this holy Immortal to tell me these things. Do you engrave them upon your hearts." The Master then retired.

On the first day of the New Year (February 2nd, 1223) the Chief Commander, the Chief Physician and the Chief Soothsayer all came to pay the compliments of the season. On the eleventh day we turned our horses' heads to the east, looking back for a moment towards Samarkand, already a thousand *li* or more behind us. We halted for a while in a large orchard. The nineteenth was the Master's birthday and all the officials burnt incense-candles and wished him long life. On the twenty-eighth Lord Li, Intendant in the Governor's office, came to say good-bye. Upon the Master's asking him whether his parting was indeed final, Li said that they would meet again in the third month. "You are ignorant," said the Master, "of Heaven's decree. In the second or third month I return to China."

On the twenty-first day we went one stage eastwards and came to a great river.[1] From here to Sairam is about three stages. The place is very fertile and well-watered; so we stayed for some time in order to refresh our oxen and horses.

On the seventh day of the second month (March 9th) the Master had an Audience and told the Khan that he had promised to be back in three years and now that the third year had come he was impatient to be back in his mountain retreat. The Emperor replied: "I am myself on my way to the east. Will you not travel with me?" The Master said he would rather go on ahead, for he had promised his friends in China to be back among them in three years. He had by now answered all the Khan's questions and earnestly desired to be dismissed. The Khan however wished him to stay for a few days more. "My sons," he said, "are soon arriving. There are still one or two points in your previous discourses which are not clear to me. When they have been explained, you may start on your journey."

On the eighth (March 11th) the Khan went hunting in the mountains to the east. He shot a boar; but at this moment his horse stumbled and he fell to the ground. Instead of rushing upon him, the boar stood perfectly still, apparently afraid to approach. In a moment his followers brought him the horse, the hunt was stopped and they all returned to the camp. Hearing of this incident the Master reproached the Emperor, telling him that in the eyes of Heaven life was a precious thing. The Khan was now well on in years and should go hunting as seldom as possible. His fall, the Master pointed out, had been a warning, just as the failure of the boar to advance and gore him had been due to the intervention of Heaven. "I know quite well," replied the Emperor, "that your advice is extremely good. But unfortunately we Mongols are brought up from childhood to shoot arrows and ride. Such a habit is not easy to lay aside. However, this time I have taken your words to heart." Then turning to *K*ishli*k* Dar*k*an he said: "In future I shall do exactly as the holy Immortal advises." It was indeed two months before he again went hunting.

Changchun, *The Travels of an Alchemist*, translated by Arthur Waley (London: Routledge and Sons, 1931), 100–101, 114–18.

[1] Probably the Chirchik.

DISCUSSION QUESTIONS

1. What prompted Chinggis to be solicitous of the Daoist Master?
2. How does the Daoist Master handle possible clashes between Mongol and Chinese values?
3. The author writes about the "great city of Samarkand" within a couple of years of its occupation by the Mongols. How does this description relate to accounts of the Mongol military campaigns against this city and other Central Asian sites?

Part IV
Expansion of the Mongol Empire

Chronicle of Novgorod

The Chronicle of Novgorod, *which spans the period from 1016 to 1471, is a valuable source of information on Russia during the Mongol era. Because Mongol forces did not occupy or devastate Novgorod, its documents and archives survived. The* Chronicle, *an ecclesiastical work, reveals Russian attitudes toward the Mongols, which were almost entirely negative and can best be characterized by the phrase "Tartar yoke." The text portrays the Mongols as destructive invaders from the East and lashes out particularly at the Tartars for damage inflicted on cities and sacred sites.*

Curiously, Novgorod was spared such damage due to Alexander Nevsky's policies. Nevsky (1221–1263), the great Russian hero who stopped a Swedish attack at the Neva River in 1240 and defeated the Teutonic knights' invasion at the Battle of the Ice in 1242, adopted a conciliatory approach toward the Mongols. Recognizing their awesome power, he maintained good relations by paying homage and sending tribute to them. He also cultivated a solid relationship with Batu Khan's son Sartakh, thus averting any Mongol attacks.

The same year, for our sins, unknown tribes came, whom no one exactly knows, who they are, nor whence they came out, nor what their language is, nor of what race they are, nor what their faith is; but they call them Tartars, and others say Taurmen, and others Pecheneg people, and others say that they are those of whom Bishop Mefodi of Patmos bore witness, that they came out from the Etrian desert which is between East and North. For thus Mefodi says, that, at the end of time, those are to appear whom Gideon scattered, and they shall subdue the whole land from the East to the Efrant [Euphrates] and from the Tigris to the Pontus sea except Ethiopia. God alone knows who they are and whence they came out. Very wise men know them exactly, who understand books; but we do not know who they are, but have written of them here for the sake of the memory of the Russian *Knyazes* and of the misfortune which came to them from them. For we have heard that they have captured many countries, slaughtered a quantity of the godless Yas, Obez, Kasog and Polovets peoples, and scattered others, who all died, killed thus by the wrath of God and of His immaculate Mother, for those cursed Polovets people had wrought much evil to the Russian Land.

* * *

And they began to organize their forces, each his own province, and they went, having collected the whole Russian Land against the Tartars, and were on the Dnieper at Zarub. Then the Tartars having learned that the Russian *Knyazes* [Princes] were coming against them sent envoys to the Russian *Knyazes:* "Behold, we hear that you are coming against us, having listened to the Polovets men; but we have not occupied your land, nor your towns, nor your villages, nor is it against you we have come. But we have come sent by God against our serfs, and our horse-herds, the pagan Polovets men, and do you take peace with us. If they escape to you, drive them off thence, and take to yourselves their goods. For we have heard that to you also they have done much harm; and it is for that reason also we are fighting them." But the Russian *Knyazes* did not listen to this, but killed all the envoys and themselves went against them, and took stand on the Dnieper, this side of Oleshe. And the Tartars sent to them envoys a second time, saying thus: "Since you have listened to the Polovets men, and have killed all our envoys, and are coming against us, come then, but we have not touched you, let God judge all."

* * *

And the Tartars turned back from the river Dnieper, and we know not whence they came, nor where they hid themselves again; God knows whence he fetched them against us for our sins.

* * *

And when the lawless ones had already come near and set up battering rams, and took the town and fired it on Friday before Sexagesima Sunday, the *Knyaz* and *Knyaginya* [Princesses] and *Vladyka* [Lords], seeing that the town was on fire and that the people were already perishing, some by fire and others by the sword, took refuge in the *Church of the Holy Mother of God* and shut themselves in the Sacristy. The pagans breaking down the doors, piled up wood and set fire to the sacred church; and slew all, thus they perished, giving up their souls to God. Others went in pursuit of *Knyaz* Yuri to Yaroslavl. And *Knyaz* Yuri sent out Dorozh to scout with 3,000 men; and Dorozh came running, and said: "They have already surrounded us, *Knyaz*." And the *Knyaz* began to muster his forces about him, and behold, the Tartars came up suddenly, and the *Knyaz*, without having been able to do anything, fled. And it happened when he reached the river Sit they overtook him and there he ended his life. And God knows how he died; for some say much about him. And Rostov and Suzhdal went each its own way. And the accursed ones having come thence took Moscow, Pereyaslavl, Yurev, Dmitrov, *Volok*, and Tver; there also they killed the son of Yaroslav. And thence the lawless ones came and invested Torzhok on the festival of the first Sunday in Lent. They fenced it all round with a fence as they had taken other towns, and here the accursed ones fought with battering rams for two weeks.

* * *

A.D. 1257. A.M. 6765

Evil news came from Russia, that the Tartars desired the *tamga* [customs tax] and tithe on Novgorod; and the people were agitated the whole year. And at Lady-day *Posadnik* [Mayor] Anani died, and in the winter the men of Novgorod killed *Posadnik* Mikhalko. If any one does good to another, then good would come of it; but digging a pit under another, he falls into it himself.

The same winter Tartar envoys came with Olexander, and Vasili fled to Pleskov; and the envoys began to ask the tithe and the *tamga* and the men of Novgorod did not agree to this, and gave presents to the *Tsar*, and let the envoys go with peace.

Chronicle of Novgorod, translated by Robert Michell and Nevill Forbes (London: Offices of the Society, 1914), 64–66, 83, 95–96.

DISCUSSION QUESTIONS

1. Compare knowledge of the Mongols found in the accounts of Juvaini and Rashid al-Din and that found in the *Chronicle of Novgorod.*
2. What did the Mongols seek from the Russians in Novgorod?
3. What would the Russians consider one of the most heinous of the Mongol crimes?

Grigor of Akanc, History of the Nation of the Archers

Grigor of Akanc offers a description of the execution of the Caliph, the most important Islamic ruler of that era. Since Grigor was born more than twenty years after the Caliph's death, this description is suspect. However, it gained wide currency throughout the known world.

See the headnote on p. 25. for additional information on this text.

After this they convened a great assembly of old and young horsemen, including the Georgian and Armenian cavalry, and with countless multitudes they moved on the city of Baghdad. When they arrived on the spot they took at once the great and famous city of Baghdad, filled with many people and rare treasures, and countless gold and silver. When they took it they slaughtered mercilessly and made many prisoners. They loaded all of the cavalry with valuable raiment and the Caliphate's gold. They seized the Caliph, the lord of Baghdad, with all of his treasures and brought him, corpulent and pot-bellied, before Hulawu. When Hulawu saw him he asked,

"Are you the lord of Baghdad?" He answered, "Yes, I am." Then he ordered him thrown into prison for three days without bread or water. After three days he ordered him brought before him (Hulawu), and Hulawu asked the Caliph, "What kind of person are you?" He answered angrily, as though to frighten Hulawu, and said, "Is this your humanity that I have been living in hunger for three days?" Previously the Caliph had told the citizens: "Be not afraid; even should the Tat'ars come, I shall bear the standard of Mahmet (Muhammad) through the gates so the Tat'ar horsemen shall all flee, and we shall be saved." Hulawu heard this and was very angry. Then he ordered a plate of red gold brought and put before *him*. When they brought it, the Caliph asked, "What is this?" Hulawu said, "This is gold; eat so thy hunger and thirst shall pass and thou shalt be assuaged." The Caliph retorted, "Man is not saved by gold, but by bread, meat, and wine." Hulawu said to the Caliph, "Since thou knowest that man is not saved by dry gold, but by bread, meat, and wine, why didst thou not send so much gold to me? Then I would not have come to plunder thy city and seize thee. But thou, without care for thyself, satest eating and drinking." Then Hulawu ordered him given to the feet of his troops, and thus to slay the Caliph of the Arabs. They (the Tat'ars) returned with much treasure and plunder to the eastern country.

* * *

Then the messengers of Manku Γan, who had come with a great (y)asax, showed Hulawu Γan great honor. There was peace for a time. Hulawu Khan was very good, loving Christians, the church, and priests. Likewise his blessed wife Tawvus Xat'un, who was good in every way, and was compassionate to the poor and needy. She very much loved all Christians, Armenians and Syrians, so that *her* tent was a church, and a sounder traveled with her, and many Armenian and Syrian priests.

The pious King of the Armenians, Het'um, heard that Hulawu Γan had been enthroned, and that he was so friendly and pro-Christian; then the Armenian King himself also went to the east with many gifts. He saw Hulawu Γan, and when the Khan saw the King of Armenia he liked him very much and honored him.

* * *

When Hulawu Γan realized that God had given him the Khanate, riches, a multitude of foot and horse soldiers and of all possessions, then he ordered a palace erected for himself at great expense on the plain of Darn, which place in their own language they called Alataγ, which had previously been the place of the summer residence of the great Armenian kings, i.e., the Arshakids. Hulawu Γan himself was of a great mind and great soul, just, and quite learned. He was a great shedder of blood, but he slew only the wicked and his enemies, and not the good or righteous. He loved the Christian folk more than the infidels. He liked the Christians so much that he took pigs for the one yearly tribute from the Armenians—100,000 shoats, and he sent two thousand pigs to every Arab city, and ordered Arab swineherds appointed to wash them every Saturday with a piece of soap, and in addition *to give them* fodder every morning, and at evening to give the pigs almonds and dates to eat. Every Arab man, were he great or small, who did not eat the flesh of swine was decapitated. So he honored the Arabs.

* * *

He began to rebuild the devastated places, and from each inhabited village he selected householders, one from the small, and two or three from the large *villages*, and he called them iam, and sent them to all of the destroyed places to undertake rebuilding. They paid no taxes at all, but *gave* only bread and broth for Tat'ar travelers. He established by such ordinances the throne of his Khanate, and he himself sate, eating and drinking with great cheer.

Grigor of Akanc, "History of the Nation of the Archers," translated by Robert Blake and Richard Frye, *Harvard Journal of Asiatic Studies* 13.3–4 (1949): 333, 335, 341, 343, 344.

DISCUSSION QUESTIONS

1. Why would this Armenian historian disparage the caliph?
2. What evidence do we have for this dialogue between the caliph and Hülegü?
3. Why would Hülegü appreciate depiction of himself as a patron of Christians?
4. What was the significance of Hülegü's reconstruction of devastated places?

Marco Polo, The Description of the World

Marco Polo (1254–1324) was the most famous traveler in world history. Accompanying his father and uncle on their second trip to the East, he reached China at the age of twenty-one. He remained at Khubilai Khan's court for sixteen years before returning to Europe. On his return journey, the Genoese, commercial enemies of the Venetians, captured him and placed him in a cell with a storyteller named Rusticello who actually wrote the book associated with Marco. The Venetian traveler devoted most of his work to China, describing the khan's palaces in Shangdu (known to the poet Samuel Taylor Coleridge as "Xanadu"), the imperial hunts, the selection of the khan's concubines, intrigues at the court involving the finance minister Ahmad, and the pony express system that conveyed Khubilai's messages to his commanders and officials at the rate of 250 miles a day. Although he exaggerated his own importance at Khubilai's court and omitted descriptions of such Chinese customs as bound feet, the character-based written language, and chopsticks, he clearly did reach China, which is confirmed by the extraordinary detail he provides about numerous incidents at court and about many Chinese cities.

En route to China, Marco visited and provided descriptions of the cities, states, and oases through which he voyaged. Some of these portraits indicate that he was gullible and accepted many local myths and legends, but his description of the Order of the Assassins has a semblance of reality.

Now I shall tell you all his doings and the life this Old Man led according as I Master Marc Pol heard it told by several men of these countries. Now they said that the Old Man was called in their language Alaodin and was with all the people over whom he ruled a follower of the law of Mahomet. He thought moreover of an unheard-of wickedness, that he should make men into bold murderers or swordsmen, who are commonly called assassins, by whose courage he might kill whoever he wished and be feared by all. He dwelled in a most noble valley shut in between two very high mountains where he had made them make the largest garden & the most beautiful that ever was seen in this world. There are abundance and delight of all the good plants, flowers, and fruits of the world, and trees which he had been able to find. And here he had made [them] make the most beautiful houses and the most beautiful palaces that ever were seen, of wonderful variety, for they were all gilded and adorned in azure very well with all the fair things of the world, both with beasts and with birds, and the hangings all of silk. And besides he had made them make in that garden many beautiful fountains which corresponded on different sides of these palaces, & all these had little conduits there, for each one, through which ran that which they threw up; through some of which it was seen ran wine & through some milk & through some honey & through some the clearest water. There were set to dwell ladies & damsels the most beautiful in the world, who all knew very well how to play on all instruments & sing tunefully & sweetly dance better than other women of this world round these fountains, so that it was a delight, & above all trained in making all the dalliance & allurements to men that can be imagined. Their duty was to furnish the young men who were put there with all delights & pleasures. There was plenty of garments, couches, food, & all things which can be desired. No sad thing was spoken of there, nor was it lawful to have time for anything but play, love, & pleasure. And these damsels most beautifully dressed in gold & silk were seen going sporting continually through the garden & through the palaces; for the women who waited on them remained shut up & were never seen abroad in the air. And the Old Man made his men understand that in that garden was Paradise. And for this reason he had it made in such a way, that Mahomet in his time made the Saracens understand about it that those who did his will should all when they died go to Paradise where they would find all the delights and pleasures of the world and will have there as many fair women as they wish at their pleasure and that they will find there beautiful gardens & full of rivers which run separately in fullness of wine and of milk and of honey and of water, in the same way as that of the Old Man; and therefore had he made them make that garden like the Paradise of which Mahomet had spoken to the Saracens. And therefore the Saracens of that country believe truly that that garden is Paradise, because of its beauty & delectable pleasure. He wished to give them to understand that he was a prophet and companion of

Mahomet, and that he could make whoever he wished go into the said Paradise. And into this garden entered no man ever except only those base men of evil life whom he wished to make satellites and assassins. Because he had indeed a castle at the entry of that garden at the mouth of the valley so very strong and impregnable that he was not afraid of a man in the world; and it could be entered by a secret way; and it was very carefully guarded, and in other parts it was not possible to enter into this garden but only there. And the Old Man kept with him at his court all the young men of the inhabitants of those mountains of the country from twelve years to twenty; they were those who seemed to wish to be men of arms and brave and valiant, who knew well by hearsay, according as Mahomet their most unhappy prophet had told them, that their Paradise was made in such manner as I have told you, and so they believed in truth as Saracens believe it. And every day he preached to them of this garden of Mahomet, and how he was able to make them go therein. And what shall I tell you about it? Sometimes the Old Man, when he wished to kill any lord who made war or was his enemy, made them put some of these youths into that Paradise by fours and sixes and by tens or twelves and by twenties together just as he wished, in this way. For he had opium to drink given them by which they fell asleep and as if half dead immediately as soon as they had drunk it, and they slept quite three days and three nights. Then he had them taken in this sleep and put into that garden of his, into different rooms of the said palaces, and there made them wake, and they found themselves there.

Marco Polo, *The Description of the World*, translated by A. C. Moule and Paul Pelliot (London: George Routledge & Sons, 2 vols., 1938), 41-42.

DISCUSSION QUESTIONS

1. Compare Marco's description of the Order of the Assassins with that of the Chinese traveler Changchun.
2. Can Marco's description be accepted as reliable? Why or why not?

Rashid al-Din, Compendium of Chronicles

Rashid al-Din offers still another description of the Mongols' campaigns in West Asia and of the defeat of the Caliph's forces. Some exaggerations may have intruded here as well.

See the headnote on p. 59 for additional information on this text.

On the 10th of Sha'ban 654 [September 2, 1256] he [Hülägü] reached Kharraqan and Bistam, and he sent the *shahna* of Herat, Märkitäi, with Beglämish on a mission to deliver threats of violence to Ruknuddin Khwarshah. At that time Mawlana Sa'id Khwaja Nasîruddin Tusi, the most learned and most intelligent man in the world, and a group of great physicians like Ra'isuddawla, Muwaffaquddawla, and their sons, who were trapped involuntarily in that land, when they saw how erratic Khwarshah's behavior was and that aggression and tyranny were part of the very fibre of his being and his madness was quite apparent, not only had wearied of but actually began to detest serving the Heretics and were desirous of helping Hülägü Khan. Prior to this they had been supportive of such an action, and they had discussed in secret amongst themselves how easy it would be for the kingdom to fall to him. Many poor people and Muslims had joined them, and they were all in full agreement in making efforts to encourage Khwarshah to surrender or to make him fear the consequences if he did not. He gave in, honored the leader of the emissaries, and sent his younger brother Shahanshah and Khwaja Asiluddin Zozani to Hülägü's court with a group of dignitaries of the realm. To encourage them to submit Hülägü ordered them shown honor and favor. Once again he assigned emissaries to go to Khwarshah with Sadruddin, Zahiruddin, Tüläk Bahadur Bakhshi, and Mazuq to say that if he was really in obedience, he should destroy his fortresses and come to court himself. In reply Khwarshah said, "If my father rebelled, I will be obedient," and he had parts of several strongholds like Maymun Diz, Alamut, and Lammasar destroyed, their battlements thrown down, their gates taken away, and the rampart walls razed. For coming out, however, he requested a one-year respite.

Since Hülägü knew that the time for Khwarshah's downfall had come and that exchanges of emissaries would not serve to threaten him further, he mounted in Bistam on the 10th of Sha'ban 654 [September 2, 1256] and set out for their lands and castles. He also gave an order for the troops in Persia and other parts to ready themselves. In the right wing went Buqa Temür and Kökä Elgäi via Mazanderan, and in the left went Tägüdär Oghul and Ket Buqa Noyan via Khwar and Simnan. Hülägü Khan was in the center, which the Mongols call *qol*, with ten thousand renowned warriors.

They set forth, and the face of the earth
turned dark. By the dust of horsemen the
celestial sphere was blinded.

Once again emissaries were sent in advance to announce that the expedition was in motion. If Khwarshah would come out, his offenses notwithstanding, he would be pardoned.

* * *

He [Hülägü] sent Sadruddin to supervise the handing over of all the strongholds and fortifications his fathers and forefathers had acquired over time in Quhistan, Rodbar, and Qumis, and which were filled to the brim with vessels and treasures. The number came to a hundred. The castellans were made to come out, and all the fortresses were razed except for Gird Koh and Lammasar. His kinsmen and adherents held Lammasar for a year. After that, pestilence broke out and many died. Those who were left came out and joined the others. They held Gird Koh for nearly twenty years, but in the end, during Abaqa Khan's reign, they came out and were killed, and it too was taken over.

In short, Khwarshah had all his adherents come out of Maymun Diz, and he presented all the hoards of buried treasure he had inherited and acquired, although they did not measure up to their reputation. The padishah distributed them among the commanders and soldiers.

Then the imperial banners proceeded from there to the foot of Alamut. Ruknuddin was sent to the foot of the fortress to get them out. The commandant resisted at first. Hülägü Khan stationed Balagha at the perimeter, and there were skirmishes for two or three days. After that, a writ of amnesty was sent, and on Saturday the 26th of Dhu'l-Qa'da [December 15] the commandant came down and surrendered the fortress. The Mongols went up, broke the catapults, and removed the gates. The inhabitants requested a three-day respite in order to remove their belongings. On the fourth day the soldiers went in and pillaged. Hülägü Khan went up on top to study Alamut, and he was amazed by the enormity of the mountain. After looking at it, he came down and decamped.

He settled in for the winter in the vicinity of Lammasar. Several days later he assigned Dayir Buqa and a troop to lay siege. On the 16th of Dhu'l-Hijja 654 [January 4, 1257], he withdrew. On Monday the 25th [January 13] he dismounted in the great *ordu* seven leagues from Qazwin to celebrate the new year *(künyanglamishi)*. Banquets were held for a week, and the princes and commanders were rewarded.

* * *

An emissary was sent to the caliph bearing threats and promises, saying, "When the Heretics' fortresses were conquered we sent emissaries to request assistance from you. In reply you said that you were in submission, but you did not send troops. Now, a token of submissiveness and allegiance is that you assist us with troops when we ride against foes. You have not done so, and you send excuses. No matter how ancient and grand your family may be, and no matter how fortunate your dynasty has been, 'is the brightness of the moon such that it can eclipse the brilliance of the sun?' Talk of what the Mongol army has done to the world and those in it from the time of Genghis Khan until today may have reached your hearing from common and elite, and you may have heard how, through God's strength, they have brought low the dynasties of the Khwarazmians, the Seljuqs, the Daylamite kings, the Atabegs, and others, all of whom were families of might and majesty. The gates of Baghdad were not closed to any of those groups, and they kept thrones there. With the might and power we possess, how shall they be closed to us?

"Previously we have given you advice, but now we say you should avoid our wrath and vengeance. Do not try to overreach yourself or accomplish the impossible, for you will only succeed in harming yourself. The past is over. Destroy your ramparts, fill in your moats, turn the kingdom over to your son, and come to us. If you do not wish to come, send all three, the vizier, Sulaymanshah, and the Dawatdar, that they may convey our message word for word. If our command is obeyed, it will not be necessary for us to wreak vengeance, and you may retain your lands, army, and subjects. If you do not heed our advice and dispute with us, line up your soldiers and get ready for the field of battle, for we have our loins girded for battle with you and are standing at the ready. When I lead my troops in wrath against Baghdad, even if you hide in the sky or in the earth, 'I shall bring you down from the turning celestial sphere; I shall pull you up like a lion. / I shall not leave one person alive in your realm, and I shall put your city and country to the torch.'

"If you desire to have mercy on your ancient family's heads, heed my advice. If you do not, let us see what God's will is."

When the emissaries arrived in Baghdad and delivered this message, the caliph sent back Sharafuddin Ibn al-Jawzi, an eloquent man, and Badruddin Muhammad Dizbaki Nakhjiwani in the company of the emissaries. In reply the caliph said, "Young man, you have just come of age and have expectations of living forever. You have seen your 'ten days' pass prosperously and auspiciously in dominating the whole world. You think your command is absolute. Since you are not going to get anything from me, why do you seek? 'You come with strategy, troops, and lasso, but how are you going to capture a star?' Does the prince not know that from the east to the west, from king to beggar, from old to young, all who are God-fearing and God-worshipping are servants of this court and soldiers in my army? When I motion for all those who are dispersed to come together, I will deal first with Iran and then turn my attention to Turan, and I will put every one in his proper place. Of course, the face of the earth will be full of tumult, but I do not seek vengeance or to harm anyone. I do not desire that the tongues of my subjects should either congratulate or curse me because of the movement of armies, especially since I am of one heart and one tongue with the Qa'an and Hülägü. If, like me, you were to sow seeds of friendship, do you think you would have to deal with my moats and ramparts and those of my servants? Adopt the path of friendship and go back to Khurasan. If you are intent upon war and battle,

Tarry not, hasten away, and abide not. If you have a moment's thought of war, / I have thousands and thousands of cavalry and infantry worthy of the battlefield,

and when they wreak vengeance they can stir up dust from the water of the sea."

Giving them a message like this, he sent the emissaries off with a few gifts and presents.

* * *

Envoys went to the city, and the next day the vizier, the divan chief, and a group of well-known citizens came out, but they were sent back. Fierce battle was fought for six days and nights. Hülägü Khan ordered six decrees written, saying, "The lives of cadis, scholars, shaykhs, Alids, and Nestorian priests, and persons who do not combat against us are safe from us." The proclamations were fastened to arrows and shot into the city from six sides. Since there was no stone in the Baghdad vicinity, they brought rocks from Jalula and Jabal Khamrin, and date palms were cut down and hurled instead of stones.

On Friday the 25th of Muharram [February 1] the Ajami Tower was destroyed. On Monday the 27th [February 3] the Mongol soldiers proceeded overwhelmingly against the ramparts opposite the Ajami Tower in the direction the padishah was. They emptied the tops of the walls of people, but they still had not gone on the walls in the direction of Suq Sultan, where Balagha and Tutar were. Hülägü Khan chastised them. Their liege men went up, and by evening they had secured the whole of the tops of the eastern walls.

When bridges were being made, Hülägü had ordered bridges built above and below Baghdad, boats made ready, catapults installed, and guards stationed. Buqa Temür and a *tümän* of soldiers were patrolling the routes to Madayin and Basra to prevent anyone from escaping by boat.

When the battle of Baghdad became intense, and the people were being pressed, the Dawatdar got in a boat to escape down river. When he passed the village of al-'Uqab, Buqa Temür let loose a barrage of catapult stones, arrows, and vials of naphtha. Three boats were taken, and the people were killed. The Dawatdar turned back in rout.

When the caliph was apprised of the situation he despaired totally of his rule of Baghdad. Seeing no escape route, he said, "I will surrender." He sent Fakhruddin Damghani and Ibn Durnus out with a few gifts, thinking that if he sent too much it would indicate how afraid he was and the foe would be further emboldened. Hülägü Khan paid no attention to the embassy, and they returned in failure.

* * *

On Friday the 9th of Safar [February 15] Hülägü Khan went into the city to see the caliph's palace. He settled into the Octagon Palace and gave a banquet for the commanders. Summoning the caliph, he said, "You are the host, and we are the guests. Bring whatever you have that is suitable for us." The caliph, thinking he was speaking seriously, trembled in fear. He was so frenzied that he couldn't tell the keys to the treasuries one from another and had to have several locks broken. He brought two thousand suits of clothing, ten thousand dinars, precious items, jewel-encrusted vessels, and several gems. Hülägü Khan paid no attention and gave it all away to the commanders and others present.

"The possessions you have on the face of the earth are apparent," he said to the caliph. "Tell my servants what and where your buried treasures are." The caliph confessed that there was a pool full of gold in the middle of the palace. They dug it up, and it was full of gold, all in hundred-mithcal ingots.

An order was given for the caliph's harem to be counted. There were seven hundred women and concubines and a thousand servants. When the caliph was apprised of the count of the harem, he begged and pleaded, saying, "Let me have the women of the harem, upon whom neither the sun nor the moon has ever shone."

"Of these seven hundred, choose a hundred," he was told, "and leave the rest." The caliph selected a hundred women from among his favorites and close relatives and took them away.

That night Hülägü Khan went to the *ordu*. The next morning he ordered Su'unchaq to go into the city, confiscate the caliph's possessions, and send them out. The items that had been accumulated over six hundred years were all stacked in mountainous piles around the *kiriyäs*. Most of the holy places like the caliph's mosque, the Musa-Jawad shrine, and the tombs in Rusafa were burned.

* * *

Ket Buqa Noyan Goes to Egypt, Does Battle with the Egyptian Army, and Is Killed

When Hülägü Khan departed from Syria, he sent a Mongol emissary with forty liege men on a mission to Egypt, saying, "God the great has elevated Genghis Khan and his progeny and given us the realms of the face of the earth altogether. Everyone who has been recalcitrant in obeying us has been annihilated along with his women, children, kith and kin, towns, and servants, as has surely reached the hearing of all. The reputation of our innumerable army is as well known as the stories of Rustam and Isfandiar. If you are in submission to our court, send tribute, come yourself, and request a *shahna*; otherwise be prepared for battle."

At that time there was no one left of Kamilite lineage worthy of ruling, and a Turcoman had become ruler. When he died he left an infant child named Muhammad, who was elevated to his father's position with Quduz as his *atabeg*. Muhammad died suddenly, and Quduz became ruler. He curried favor with the people through largesse. Most of the soldiers of Syria and Egypt were the defeated troops of Sultan Jalaluddin who had fled from the gates of Akhlat and gone to Syria. Their leaders and commanders were Barakat Khan and Malik Ikhtiyaruddin Khan son of . . . , and Malik Sayfuddin Sadiq Khan son of Mingbuqa, Malik Nasiruddin Güshlü Khan son of Beg Arslan, Atlas Khan, and Nasiruddin Muhammad Qaymari. When Hülägü Khan set out for Syria, they went into hiding in the surrounding areas, and after he pulled out, they reassembled and headed for Cairo in Egypt, where they told their sad story to Quduz. He showed them favor, sympathized with them, and gave them much money. They all became wholehearted supporters of Quduz' rule.

When the emissaries arrived, Quduz summoned them and consulted with them on what to do, saying, "Hülägü Khan has proceeded from Turan with a huge army into Iran, and no one, caliph, sultan, or malik, has the ability to withstand his onslaught. Having conquered all lands, he has come to Damascus, and were it not for the news of his brother's death he would have added Egypt to his conquests too. In addition, he has stationed in this area Ket Buqa Noyan, who is like a raging lion and fire-breathing dragon lying in ambush. If he attacks Egypt, no one will be able to contend with him. Before we lose all power of self-determination, we must come up with a strategy."

"In addition to being Genghis Khan's grandson, Tolui Khan's son, and Mänggü Qa'an's brother," said Nasiruddin Qaymari, "Hülägü Khan has power and might beyond description. At present he holds from the gates of Egypt to the borders of China in his mighty grasp, and he has been singled out for heavenly assistance. If we go before him under amnesty, it will not be blameworthy. However, willingly to drink poison and to go out to greet one's own death are far from the path of wisdom. A human being is not a grape vine that doesn't mind having its head cut off. He does not keep his word, for with no warning he killed Khwarshah, Musta'sim, Husamuddin Akka, and the lord of Arbela after having made promises to them. If we go to him he will do the same to us."

"At the present time," said Quduz, "everywhere in Diyarbekir, Diyar Rabi'a, and Greater Syria is filled with lamentation. The land from Baghdad to Anatolia lies in ruins, devoid of farmers and seed. If we don't make a pre-emptive strike and try to repulse them, soon Egypt will be destroyed like the others. Given the multitudes with which he is proceeding in our direction, one of three things must be done: we must make a truce, offer resistance, or go into exile. Exile is impossible, for there is nowhere we can go other than North Africa, and a bloodthirsty desert and vast distances lie between us and there."

"A truce is also imprudent," said Nasiruddin Qaymari, "for their word is not to be trusted."

The other commanders said, "We do not have the power to resist either. You must say what you think the best plan is."

"My opinion," said Quduz, "is that we go out to battle together. If we win, fine; otherwise, we will not suffer blame from the people."

After that, the amirs agreed, and Quduz consulted with Bunduqdar, his chief amir, in private. "My opinion," said Bunduqdar, "is that we should kill the emissaries and ride as one to attack Ket Buqa. Win or die, in either case we will not be blamed, and we will have people's gratitude."

Quduz approved this plan, and by night he had the emissaries crucified. The next morning they perforce committed themselves to battle and mounted. Amir Baidar, who was the leader of the Mongol *yäzäk* [advance troop], sent a man named Aghlabak to Ket Buqa Noyan to inform him of the movement of the Egyptian troops. Ket Buqa sent in reply, "Stay where you are and wait for me."

Before Ket Buqa arrived, Quduz attacked Baidar and drove him to the banks of the Orontes. Ket Buqa Noyan, his zeal stirred, flared up like fire with all confidence in his own strength and might. Quduz stationed his troops in ambush and, himself mounted with a few others, stood waiting. He clashed with Ket Buqa and his several thousand cavalry, all experienced warriors, at Ayn Jalut. The Mongols attacked, raining down arrows, and Quduz pulled a feint and started to withdraw. Emboldened, the Mongols lit out after him, killing many of the Egyptians, but when they came to the ambush spot, the trap was sprung from three sides. A bloody battle ensued, lasting from dawn till midday. The Mongols were powerless to resist, and in the end they were put to flight.

Ket Buqa Noyan kept attacking left and right with all zeal. Some encouraged him to flee, but he refused to listen and said, "Death is inevitable. It is better to die with a good name than to flee in disgrace. In the end, someone from this army, old or young, will reach the court and report that Ket Buqa, not wanting to return in shame, gave his life in battle. The padishah should not grieve over lost Mongol soldiers. Let him imagine that his soldiers' wives have not been pregnant for a year and the mares of their herds have not foaled. May felicity be upon the padishah. When his noble being is well, every loss is compensated. The life or death of servants like us is irrelevant." Although the soldiers left him, he continued to struggle in battle like a thousand men. In the end his horse faltered, and he was captured.

Near the battlefield was a reed bed in which a troop of Mongol cavalrymen was hiding. Quduz ordered fire thrown into it, and they were all burned alive. After that, Ket Buqa was taken before Quduz with his hands bound.

"Despicable man," said Quduz, "you have shed so much blood wrongfully, ended the lives of champions and dignitaries with false assurances, and overthrown ancient dynasties with broken promises. Now you have finally fallen into a snare yourself."

When the one whose hands were bound
heard these words, he reared up like a mad
elephant / And replied, saying, "O proud
one, do not pride yourself on this day of victory."

"If I am killed by your hand," said Ket Buqa, "I consider it to be God's act, not yours. Be not deceived by this event for one moment, for when the news of my death reaches Hülägü Khan, the ocean of his wrath will boil over, and from Azerbaijan to the gates of Egypt will quake with the hooves of Mongol horses. They will take the sands of Egypt from there in their horses' nose bags. Hülägü Khan has three hundred thousand renowned horsemen like Ket Buqa. You may take one of them away."

Quduz said, "Speak not so proudly of the horsemen of Turan, for they perform deeds with trickery and artifice, not with manliness like Rustam."

"As long as I have lived," replied Ket Buqa, "I have been the padishah's servant, not a mutineer and regicide like you!

Let the malevolent retain neither head nor
body, for he deprives his prince of life.

Finish me off as quickly as possible." Quduz ordered his head severed from his body.

* * *

Around then emissaries arrived from Cathay to announce that Qubilai Qa'an was on the throne and that Ariq Bökä was in obedience to him. Alghu was dead, and Hülägü was commanded to rule from the Oxus to the farthest reaches of Syria and Egypt. Thirty thousand Mongol horsemen had been sent to reinforce him. Noqai took fright at these words and turned pale. Tucking his tail between his legs, he said nothing more. Shaykh Sharif came to Hülägü Khan's court and reported, and Hülägü Khan rewarded him and filled the world with justice and equity.

The History of the End of Hülägü Khan's Reign; Abaqa Khan Is Sent to Khurasan; the Provinces Are Transferred to the Commanders and Governors; Hülägü's Illness and Death

Hülägü Khan loved to build, and many of the edifices he had constructed still remain. He built a palace in Ala Tagh and a temple in Khoy. In that year he occupied himself with construction projects and civil and military administration. When autumn came he set out for his winter quarters at the Zarina, which the Mongols call Jaghatu and Naghatu. He went to Maragha, where he was insistent that the observatory be completed. A great lover of wisdom, he encouraged the learned to debate the basic sciences and rewarded them all with stipends and salaries. His court was adorned by the presence of philosophers and scientists. He was exceptionally fond of the science of alchemy, and its practitioners received extraordinary patronage from him. According to their own delusions and fancies they lit fires, burned innumerable potions, and spouted a lot of useless hot air to young and old alike about making "pots of the clay of wisdom," but the benefit of it reached nothing but their nostrils and palates. In transmutation they had no luck, but they were miracles of cheating and fraud, squandering and wasting the stores of the workshops of lordly power. In supplying them, meeting their demands, and paying their salaries, more was spent than Qarun made by alchemy in his whole life.

Rashid al-Din, *Compendium of Chronicles*, translated by Wheeler Thackston (Cambridge: Harvard University Department of Near Eastern Languages and Civilizations, 3 vols., 1998), 483, 485, 488–89, 496, 498, 504–06, 512–13.

DISCUSSION QUESTIONS

1. Describe how Hülegü used a blend of threats and actual attacks in his dealings with the "Heretics" (Order of the Assassins). How would such a policy benefit him in future campaigns?
2. How did Hülegü's justifications for his attack on the caliph of the Abbasid dynasty differ from Chinggis's justifications for attacks on other states? Is he referring to the Mongols' Sky God when he says, "God the eternal elevated Genghis Khan" [Chinggis Khan]? Or is he referring to another god?
3. Why would Hülegü note that he would not harm scholars, judges, Nestorian priests, Shaykhs, "and persons who do not combat us"?
4. What did the Mongols choose as booty from the caliph?
5. Why did the lack of a regular and orderly system of succession to the position of Great Khan undermine the Mongols?
6. The battle of Ayn Jalut was a minor engagement. Why did it prove to be so significant?
7. What is the evidence for and significance of contacts between Hülegü and the other Mongol rulers of the Middle East and the Yuan dynasty of China?
8. Why would Hülegü indicate that he would provide support for astronomers, philosophers, and scientists?

Baybars I of Egypt

Baybars I (1223–1277) was a Turkic soldier who rose to become the sultan of the Mamluk dynasty. He first gained renown during the Seventh Crusade, which King Louis (St. Louis) of France launched in Egypt. His forces defeated Louis, and the Mamluks then captured and ransomed him for a large sum. He continued to climb the ranks of military commanders until his greatest triumph, the defeat of the Mongols at Ayn Jalut in 1260. In the same year, Sultan Qutuz was assassinated in a conspiracy that probably involved Baybars. He then assumed the title of sultan and strove until his death to unite Egypt and Syria while at the same time defending against additional Mongol assaults and trying to root out the crusader states from the Middle East.

The sultan ascended the hill overlooking 'Ain Jalut. He and those with him stayed on horseback throughout the night, while the Mongols encamped near them. Al-Malik al-Muzaffar and the army marched on ignorant of the nearness of the enemy, till the messengers of al-Malik al-Zahir arrived and warned them, informing them of the proximity of the enemy; and they also drew their attention to the weakness of the enemy and disparaged the latter, encouraging them to take advantage of the opportunity; and this was one of the causes of the victory. Had he not undertaken to sacrifice himself, to precede and advance, and pass wakeful nights in defending the possessions (of Islam), the situation would have been—may God save us—terrible and the country would have been ruined, since the Muslims would have marched in ignorance, for the reason that the enemy had kept his whereabouts secret; but the intelligence sent by him preceded the enemy.

When the armies reached the sultan, he stood before the enemy and bore the first shock of their onslaught. The enemy saw his bravery, the like of which was never heard of before. The Muslims saw that he stood firm among them, and so they ventured against the enemy and drove onward. Al-Malik al-Muzaffar and the Atabek advanced with the banners, and so God had ordained the victory, which was due to al-Malik al-Zahir. When the enemy, having been put to flight, climbed up the mountain, al-Malik al-Zahir followed on foot and stood facing the enemy all day long till nightfall. People everywhere heard about his stand on the mountain, and they climbed up to him from every direction, while he was fighting like one who staked his very life. The foot-soldiers bagan to climb up and collect the heads of those whom he killed and who were killed in front of him, and they carried heads of such persons as Kitbugha Nowin and others to al-Malik al-Muzaffar. Before the day passed, a great number of heads had been gathered before al-Malik al-Muzaffar. When al-Malik al-Zahir came down he did not heed the fatigue which he had suffered, but rode on and pressed after the enemy, his men following him. He did not cease to ride night and day, without rest, killing or taking captive those who were unwounded, while the enemy was put to flight before him. He did not draw rein until he reached Harim. When he reached Afamiyah the enemy rallied again; and he again inflicted a smashing defeat on them at Afamiyah on Friday, and their wealth, women, children and horses were plundered.

In the meantime he had sent to Damascus an emissary who ensured its safety and tranquillity and informed the people of the victory over the enemy, and gave instructions to them regarding the enemy, and ordered them to kill the deputies and slaves of the enemy and not to pay any attention to them, and to be cautious lest the deputies of the enemy should despoil the country or any of the people. Al-Malik al-Muzaffar (mercy be on him) went with all his army, and they found that our master the sultan (may God grant him victory) had put the affairs of the territories in order for them and resettled the rest of the subjects there, and encouraged his men to advance. Al-Malik al-Muzaffar reached Damascus without fatigue or hardship. Letters from our master the sultan reached al-Malik al-Muzaffar at Damascus, informing him of his activities, conquests and plans, and also stating that he had sent the amir 'Imad al-din Abu Bakr b. al-Mujir to Aleppo, and had made some appointments in the various territories; that there remained no enemy in front of him in Syria and at Aleppo and he had sent some men to Hamah and Hims and other places, to ensure tranquillity and safety there.

* * *

Sending of Ambassadors to King Bereke

When, the first group of Mongols having come to the sultan, he had acquainted himself with the state of affairs from them, and realised the strength of Bereke [of Golden Horde], the place of his residence, and the way which led into his country; he dispatched the ambassadors, as we have said before, and sent with them two men from among the above-mentioned Mongols who were the servants and associates of the king, and who knew the country. He placed a friendly letter in the hands of the ambassadors, inviting him into an alliance and urging him to undertake holy war, and giving a description of the Muslim armies, their great number, and the variety of peoples included in them, comprising horsemen, Turkomans, Kurdish tribes and Bedouin tribes; (giving a description of) the Muslim and Frankish kings who obeyed Egypt, who disagreed with her, who were in agreement with her and offered presents to her and made truce with her; stating that all of them were submissive and obedient to his orders, and saying other things to incite Bereke against Hulagu (may God disgrace him), belittling the latter's importance, instigating opposition to him; and saying that negligence in this matter would be shameful; making him understand that whatever Hulagu did was intended as a defiance against Bereke; and informing him in the letter of the arrival of a group of Mongols who claimed that they were his partisans, and that they had received favourable welcome in consideration of him (Bereke). Then he sent with this envoy the amir Kusharbak, who was a Turk and had been a Jamadar of Khwarizm Shah, and knew the country and the language, and the jurist Majd al-din al-Rawdhrawari, to accompany the two Mongols. The sultan equipped them and embarked them in a transport vessel, giving them provisions for many months. One of them read the letter out twice in front of all the amirs in the hall. Then our master the caliph came, and the oath of allegiance was taken before them, the ambassadors also taking the oath of allegiance to him. Then they attended his sacred khutba, and were introduced to him. The sultan charged them verbally concerning matters relating to the interest of Islam, and urged them to acquaint their Mongol companions with the condition of his armies and their large number, the activity which he undertook for holy war, his service and his efforts in aid of the Faith and the wars with the polytheistic enemies; and he further said that he was an admirer of King Bereke and prayed for his victory over the enemy, and that he would support him in his enterprise in the interest of the world. Then these two persons started out in Muharram of the year 661 A.H. and all of them reached the territories of Michael Palaeologus, who treated them kindly. Their arrival coincided with the arrival of the ambassadors of Bereke to Michael Palaeologus, so he sent them with these people.

* * *

When the sultan settled himself in the Citadel, he gave them audience in the presence of the amirs and the people, and read the letters brought by the amir Jalal al-din and the Shaikh Nur al-din, which contained blessings, thanks, a request for help against Hulagu, and information about Bereke's disagreement with Sunkur Khan and about the creed of his people, and said that Sunkur Khan's activities were harmful to the people who were suffering injustice from him, and it further stated: 'I and my four brothers are fighting against him on every side, for the establishment of Islam and restoration of the abodes of right guidance which had been previously set up, and for the praise of God, the call to prayer, recitation of the Qor'an and prayer, and to avenge the deaths of imams and of the massacred people. He requested the sultan to send an army towards the Euphrates to block the way of Hulagu, and he commended Sultan 'Izz al-din, the ruler of Rum, to the sultan's favour and asked him to extend his help. Then the assembly dispersed and innumerable presents were sent to the ambassadors.

The sultan gave orders for the preparation of the presents to be sent to King Bereke, comprising all sorts of things. A banquet was given for them at Luq, and he paid visits to those two ambassadors on Saturday and Tuesday of each week when he went to play polo, with various kinds of presents and fabrics. This Mamluk (the author) wrote a reply to the letter of King Bereke on seventy sheets of half-size Baghdad paper, containing verses from the Book of God the Exalted and traditions of the Prophet (may God bless him and grant him peace) which urged holy war, and those traditions and verses which occur concerning Egypt, warfare against polytheists and the emulation of the Prophet of God (may God bless him and grant him peace) in the cause of holy war; in it were mentioned the abodes of prayer, holy places in all countries in which prayers were offered in his name, and many other things. This letter contained encouragement, warning, compliments and instigation, the sultan's greatness, a declaration of sympathy for him, the description of the vastness of the Egyptian army and what they were engaged in, and of the army's normal large size, assuring him that all of them were ready to help him for the support of Islam. I read the letter to the sultan before the amirs, and he added something to it, as well as the Atabek, who dictated it. When this letter was complete, the following presents were prepared: A Holy Qor'an, said to have been transcribed by 'Uthman b. 'Affan (may God be pleased with him) enclosed in a case of red satin embroidered with gold, over which was a leather cover lined with striped silk, and a stand for it encrusted with carved ivory and ebony with a silver latch and a silver lock; a great quantity of finished Venetian cloth, prayer carpets and other carpets of diverse colours, coloured Levantine robes, several leather cushions, leather sheets for making tents, a large number of tables intended to hold chandeliers, Qaljuri swords with silver hilts, gilded iron clubs and others, Frankish helmets with silver collars, painted shields, lamps with Venetian shades, polished bowls for candles with shades, silver lamps with Venetian shades, a sufficient number of small saws made like spears for silver lamps, a double candlestick the base of which was wholly inlaid with metal, bridles inlaid with metal, the tops being threaded through with silver-ornamented rope, silver jackets inlaid with gold, well-ornamented cruppers, felt-covers, saddles from Khwarizm complete with cushions, Russian-leather bags threaded through with strings and silver ribbons, cross-bows from Damascus with strings of silk, arbalests with their strings.

Syedeh Fatima Sadeque, ed., *Baybars I of Egypt* (Dacca: Oxford University Press, 1956), 93–94, 156–57, 187, 189.

DISCUSSION QUESTIONS

1. Assess the differences in Rashid al-Din's and Baybars's descriptions of the battle of Ayn Jalut.
2. Judging from the Mamluk sultan Baybars's and the Golden Horde's Khan Berke's alliance against the Il-Khan Hülegü, analyze the status of unity and identity among the Mongols.
3. Describe diplomatic practices in Asia during the thirteenth century.

The Letter of the Great Khan Güyüg to Pope Innocent IV

The Great Khan Güyük's letter responded to two papal bulls brought by John of Plano Carpini. The letter and the bulls yield insights into the Mongols' and the Pope's worldviews. Each refers to a different higher power to legitimize their conceptions.

By the power of the Eternal Sky, [We] the Oceanic Khan of the whole great people; Our command.

This is an order sent to the great Pope that he may know and understand it.

We have written it in the language of the lands of the *kerel* (i.e. Latin?).

Counsel was held; a petition of submission was sent; it was heard from your ambassadors.

And if you keep to your word, thou, who art the great Pope, together with all the kings, must come in person to do homage to Us. We shall then cause you to hear every command that there is of the *Yasa* ('Law').

Again. You have said: 'Become Christian, it will be good.' Thou hast made thyself wise (*or* thou hast been presumptuous); thou hast sent a petition. This petition of thine We have not understood.

Again. You have sent words [saying]: 'Thou hast taken all the lands of the Majar and the Christians; I am astonished. What was their crime? Tell us.' These words of thine We have not understood either. The command of God, Chingiz Khan and Qa'an (=Ögödei), both of them, sent it to cause it to be heard. They have not trusted the command of God. Just like thy words they too have been reckless; they have acted with arrogance; and they killed Our ambassadors. The people of those countries, [it was] the Ancient God [who] killed and destroyed them. Except by the command of God, how should anyone kill, how should [anyone] capture by his own strength?

Dost thou say none the less: 'I am a Christian; I worship God; I despise and . . .'? How dost thou know whom God forgives, to whom He shows mercy? How dost thou know, who speakest such words?

By the power of God [from] the going up of the sun to [his] going down [He] has delivered all the lands to Us; We hold them. Except by the command of God, how can anyone do [anything]? Now you must say with a sincere heart: 'We shall become [your] subjects; we shall give [our] strength.' Thou in person at the head of the kings, you must all together at once come to do homage to Us. We shall then recognize your submission. And if you do not accept God's command and act contrary to Our command We shall regard you as enemies.

Thus We inform you. And if you act contrary [thereto], what do We know [of it], [it is] God [who] knows.

In the last days of Jumada II of the year six hundred and forty-four (3–11 November 1246).

Igor de Rachewiltz, *Papal Envoys to the Great Khans* (Stanford: Stanford University Press, 1971), 213–14.

DISCUSSION QUESTION

1. Analyze the characteristics of these so-called Orders of Submission, as expressed in Güyük's letter to the Pope?

Part V
Mongol Rule

Rashid al-Din, Compendium of Chronicles

In this selection, Rashid al-Din documents a dramatic change in Mongol policy. Starting with Ögödei, the Mongols seek to rule, rather than simply to exploit, conquered territories.

See the headnote on p. 59 additional information on this text.

Between the countries of Khitai and that town other *yams*[1] were established in addition to the *tayan yams*. At every stage a *tümen* [10,000-men army] was posted for the protection of the *yams*. And he had issued a *yasa* [law] to the effect that every day five hundred wagons fully loaded with food and drink should arrive thither from the provinces to be placed in stores and then dispensed there. For [corn] and [wine] there were provided great wagons drawn by six oxen each.

He [Ögödei] ordered the Muslim *uzan*[2] to build a pavilion a day's journey from Qara-Qorum, in a place where were in ancient

[1] T. *yam*, Mo. *jam*, "post station." There were, according to the Chinese sources, three kinds of stations with the Mongol names: *morin jam*, "horse station," *tergen jam*, "wagon station," and *narin jam*, "secret station," the last-named used for urgent military matters. The *tayan yam* of Rashid al-Din—the spelling of the first element (*T*AYAN) is quite uncertain—seems to stand in opposition to the *narin jam* and so to mean something like "ordinary post station."

[2] *Uzan*: Persian plural of T. *uz*, "skillful, craftsman."

days the falconers of Afrasiyab[3] and which is called Gegen-Chaghan. He would be in this place in the spring because he used to fly hawks there. In the summer he would be in Örmügetü. There he had pitched a great tent which held a thousand persons and which was never struck. The outside was adorned with gold studs and the inside covered with *nasij*. It is called Sira-Ordo. In the autumn he was in Köke-Na'ur, 4 days' journey from Qara-Qorum, where he would remain for 40 days. His winter quarters were at Ongqïn, where he would pass his time hunting in the Bülengü and Jelingü mountains and so complete the winter. In short, his spring quarters were in the neighborhood of Qara-Qorum, his summer quarters in the meadows of Örmügetü, his autumn quarters between Köke-Na'ur and Usun-Qol, a day's journey from Qara-Qorum, and his winter quarters at Ongqïn. And when he was on his way to Qara-Qorum, there was a tall pavilion which he had built 2 parasangs from the town named Tuzghu-Balïq; here he would eat *tuzghu* from the town and make merry for one day. Then on the next day the people would don garments of one color, and he would proceed from thence to Qarshi, where tender youths would stand before him and for the space of a month he would devote himself to pleasure. He would open the doors of the treasuries and cause noble and base to share his general bounty; and every night he would pit archers, crossbowmen, and wrestlers against one another and would show favor and make presents to the winners.

In his winter quarters at Ongqïn he had ordered a wall of wood and clay, 2 days' journey in length, to be erected and gates set in it. This they called *jihik*. When hunting, the soldiers on every side were all instructed to form themselves gradually into a hunting ring and make for the wall, driving the game toward it. From a distance of a month's journey, proceeding with the utmost caution, they would slowly form themselves into a ring and drive the animals into the *jihik*, [at which point] the soldiers would stand shoulder to shoulder in a circle. Then, first of all, Ögetei Qa'an would enter the circle with

[3] Probably Bügü Khan, the legendary ruler of the Uighur, is meant. Already in the 11th century Kashghari had identified Alp-Er Tonga, a mythical Turkish hero, with Afrasiyab, the hereditary enemy of Iran in the Persian National Epic. So too the Qara-Khanids claimed to be of the "house of Afrasiyab" (*āl-i Afrāsiyāb*).

his personal retinue and amuse himself for awhile killing game. When he grew tired he would ride up on to high ground in the middle of the ring, and the princes would enter in due order; then the common people and soldiers would do their killing; then some [of the animals] would be released for breeding and the rest of the game would be distributed by the *büke'üls* [tasters] to all the various princes and emirs of the army, so that no one went without his share. All that company would perform the ceremony of *tikishmishi* [gift-giving], and then after 9 days of feasting each tribe would return to its own *yurt* and home.

Account of Qa'an's Illness and Death

Qa'an was extremely fond of wine, and [he] drank continuously and to excess. Day by day he grew weaker, and though his intimates and well-wishers sought to prevent him, it was not possible, and he drank more in spite of them. Chaghatai appointed an emir as *shahna* [governor] to watch over him and not allow him to drink more than a specified number of cups. As he could not disobey his brother's command, he used to drink from a large cup instead of a small one, so that the number remained the same. And that emir-supervisor also used to give him wine and act as a drinking companion in order to make himself one of his confidants; and so his attendance brought no benefit to Qa'an.

* * *

It is the *yasa* and *yosun* [custom] of the Mongols that in spring and summer no one may sit in water by day, nor wash his hands in a stream, nor draw water in gold and silver vessels, nor lay out washed garments upon the plain; it being their belief that such actions increase the thunder and lightning, which they greatly dread and shun. One day Qa'an had been hunting with Chaghatai, and as they were returning they beheld a Muslim sitting in midstream washing himself. Chaghatai, who was extremely precise in the enforcement of the *yasa*, wished to put the man to death. But Qa'an said: "Today it is late and we are tired. Let him be held in custody tonight, and tomorrow he can be tried and punished." He handed the man over to Danishmand Hajib, telling him in secret to have a silver *balish* thrown in the water where the man had been washing and to have him instructed to say, at the time of the trial, that he was a poor man, that all the capital he possessed had fallen into the water, and that he had plunged in in order to pull it out. On the next day, at the time of the examination, the man had recourse to this excuse, and some persons were sent to the place and found the *balish* in the water. Then Qa'an said: "Who would dare to contravene the Great Yasa? But this poor man, because of his great distress and helplessness, has sacrificed himself for this wretched amount." He pardoned him and commanded that he should be given 10 more *balish* from the treasure; and a written statement was taken from him that he would not commit a similar action again. On this account the freemen of the world became the slaves of his nature, which is better than much treasure. *Praise be to God, Lord of the worlds!*

* * *

There was a poor man who was unable to earn a living and had learnt no trade. He sharpened pieces of iron into the shape of awls and mounted them on pieces of wood. He then sat waiting where Qa'an would pass. His auspicious glance fell upon him from afar and he sent someone to inquire into his circumstances. The poor man told him that he was of feeble condition and small property and had a large family; and he had brought these awls for Qa'an. He gave the awls to that emir, who told Qa'an about him but did not show him the awls because they were so ill-made. Qa'an said; "Bring me what he has brought." And taking those awls into his auspicious hand he said: "Even this kind will serve for herdsmen to mend the seams in their kumys skins with." And for each awl, which was not worth a barley-corn, he bestowed a *balish.*

* * *

A person asked to be given 500 gold *balish* from the treasury by way of capital so that he might engage in trade. Qa'an ordered the amount to be given. His attendants pointed out that this was a man of no standing, with no money and owing debts to that amount. He ordered them to give him 1,000 *balish*, so that he might pay half to his creditors and use the other half as capital.

* * *

A stranger brought a pair of arrows and knelt down. They inquired into his circumstances and he said: "My trade is that of an arrowsmith and I have a debt of 70 *balish.* If it is commanded that I be paid this amount from the treasury I will deliver ten thousand arrows every year." Said Qa'an: "The poor fellow's affairs must be entirely distraught for him to accept these *balish* for so many arrows. Give him 100 *balish* in cash so that he can mend his affairs." The *balish* were delivered immediately, but he was unable to carry them. Qa'an laughed and commanded him to be given a yoke of oxen and a wagon also. He loaded the *balish* on the wagon and went on his way.

* * *

When the fame of his bounty and beneficence had been spread throughout the world, merchants made their way to his court from every side. He would command their wares to be bought, whether they were good or bad, and the full price paid. And it usually happened that he would give them away without having looked at them. They for their part would make their calculations [by] fixing the price of one item at that of ten.

* * *

Some people from India brought him two tusks of ivory. He asked what they wanted and was told "500 *balish*." Without the slightest hesitation he ordered them to be given this amount. The officers of the Court made a great outcry, asking how he could give so large a sum for so contemptible a matter, when these people had come from an enemy country. "No one," he replied, "is an enemy of mine. Give them the money and let them go."

Someone, at a time when he was drunk, brought him a cap of the kind worn in Persia. He ordered a draft to be written for 200 *balish*. [The secretaries] delayed [affixing] the *al-tamgha* [seal], thinking he had made such an order on account of his drunken state. The next day his glance fell upon that person. The secretaries laid [the draft] before him, and he ordered the man to be paid 300 *balish*. They held up the matter again for the same reason; and every day he increased the amount until it came to 600 *balish*. Then, summoning the emirs and *bitikchis* [secretaries], he asked them whether there was anything in the world that would endure forever. They replied with one voice that there was not. Then, addressing himself to the Minister Yalavach he said: "That is wrong, for good repute and fair fame will endure forever." To the *bitikchis* he said: "You are my real enemies, for you do not wish fair fame and a good name to remain as a memorial to me. You think that I give presents because I am drunk, and so you delay payment and hold up what is due.

Until one or two of you have been punished for [these] deeds as a warning to the rest, no good will come of you."

The Successors of Genghis Khan, translated by John Boyle (New York: Columbia University Press, 1971), 62–65, 77, 79–83.

DISCUSSION QUESTIONS

1. What was the significance of postal stations for the Mongols?
2. Why did Ögödei have several capitals?
3. Why did Ögödei accept poor quality goods from merchants?
4. What policies was Ögödei supporting with this description from Rashid al-Din? How did these accounts assist in ruling?

Marco Polo, The Description of the World

Marco Polo was a remarkably astute observer. An inquisitive young man, he learned about and reported on a wide variety of Chinese practices, innovations, and sites. In this selection, he provides Europeans with the first descriptions of paper money and of Khubilai Khan's summer palace at Shangdu (which he refers to as Ciandu and which Europeans knew as Xanadu). The city of Hangzhou (his "Quinsai") made a deep impression on him, and he writes more about it than other sites he visited.

See the headnote on p. 101 for additional information on this text.

Here he tells of the city of Ciandu and of the wonderful palace of the great kaan. And when one is set out from the city of Ciagannor which I have named to you above and one goes riding three days journeys then one finds a city which is called Ciandu, which the great Kaan, who now is and reigns and who has the name Cublai Kaan, who is spoken of in this book, made them make there. And in this city Cublai Kaan made them make there a vast palace of marble cunningly worked and of other fair stone, which with one end has its boundary in the middle of the city, and with the other with the wall of it. The halls and rooms and passages are all gilded & wonderfully painted within with pictures and images of beasts and birds and trees and flowers and many kinds of things, so well and so cunningly that it is a delight and a wonder to see. It is very wonderfully beautiful and well worked. And from this palace is built a second wall which in the direction opposite to the palace, closing one end in the wall of the city on one side of the palace and the other on the other side, encloses and surrounds quite sixteen miles of plain land in circuit, in such a way that unless one starts from the palace he cannot enter into that close; & it is fortified like a castle; in which wall are fountains and rivers of running water and very beautiful lawns and groves enough. And the great Kaan keeps all sorts of not fierce wild beasts which can be named there, & in very great numbers, that is harts and bucks and roe-deer, to give to the gerfalcons to eat and to the falcons, which he keeps in mew in that place, which are more than two hundred gerfalcons without the falcons. And he always goes himself to see them in mew at least once every week. And the great Kaan often goes riding through this park which is surrounded with a wall and takes with him one tame leopard or more on the crupper of his horse, and when he wishes he lets it go and takes one of the aforesaid animals, a hart or buck or roe-deer and has them given to the falcons and gerfalcons which he keeps in mew. And he does that often for his pleasure and for amusement. And certainly this place is so well kept & adorned that it is a most noble thing of great delight. And again you may know that in the middle place of that park thus surrounded with a wall, where there is a most beautiful grove, the great Kaan has made for his dwelling a great palace or loggia which is all of canes, upon beautiful pillars gilded and varnished, and on the top of each pillar is a great dragon all gilded which winds the tail round the pillar and holds up the ceiling with the head, and stretches out the arms, that is one to the right hand for the support of the ceiling and the other in the same way to the left; but it is all gilded inside and out and worked & painted with beasts and with birds very cunningly worked. The roof of this palace is also all of canes gilded and varnished so well and so thickly that no water can hurt it, and the paintings can never be washed out; & it is the most wonderful thing in the world to be understood by one who has not seen it; and I will tell you how it is made of canes. You may know truly that those canes of which these houses are made are more than three or four palms thick and round and are from ten paces to fifteen long. One cuts them across in half at the knot, from one knot to the other, and splits them through the middle lengthwise, and then a tile is made; and from each splitting two tiles are made. And of these canes which are thick and so large are made pillars, beams, and partitions, and they are put to many other uses, for they do many other works with them, [so] that one can roof a whole house with them and do all from the beginning,—and this palace of the great Kaan, which is in the middle of that park, of which I have told you above was all made of canes. But each tile of cane is fixed with nails for protection from the winds, and they make those canes so well set together and joined that they protect the house from rain and send the water off downwards. Moreover the great Kaan had made it so arranged that he might have it easily taken away and easily set up, put together and taken to pieces, without any harm whenever he wished, for when it is raised and put together more than two hundred very strong ropes of silk held it up in the manner of tents all round about, because owing to the lightness of the canes it would be thrown to the ground by the wind. And I tell you that the great Kaan stays there in that park three months of the year.

* * *

How the great Kaan causes sheets to be spent for money. It is true that the mint of the great lord is in this said town of Cambaluc, and it is appointed in such a way that one can well say that the great lord has the alchemy perfectly, and I shall show it you now, the reason how. Now you may know that he has such a money as I shall tell you made in this way. He makes men take the middle bark of the three barks of the trees which are called gelsus, that is of the mulberries of which the worms that make silk eat their leaves—for there are so many of them that all the country-sides are loaded and full of these said trees, and they take the thin skin which is between the thick outer bark and the wood of the tree and is white, and they grind it and pound it and of that thin skin he makes them make then with glue sheets like those of cotton paper, and they are all black. And when these sheets are made he has them cut up in this fashion—in large portions and small, and they are forms of money, square and more long than broad. For he makes a little one which is worth in their manner about a half of a small tornesel, and the next, a little larger, is of one tornesel, also small, and the next, a little larger, is of a half Venetian groat of silver, and the next of a groat of silver which is worth a silver groat of Venese, and the next is of two Venetian groats, & the next of five Venetian groats, and the next of ten groats, and the next of one bezant of gold, and the next two bezants of gold, and the next of three bezants of gold, and the next four bezants of gold, and the next five bezants of gold, and so it goes up to ten bezants of gold. And all these sheets [or] moneys are sealed with the mark and with the seal of the great lord, for otherwise they could by no means be spent. And they are made with as much authority and formality as if they were of pure gold or silver, for many officials who are deputed for this write their names on every coin, placing there each one his mark, and when it is all done as it ought to be, the head of them deputed by the lord stains the seal entrusted to him with cinnabar and impresses it upon the coin so that the pattern of the seal dipped in the cinnabar remains printed there, and then that money is authorised. And if anyone were to counterfeit it he would be punished with the last penalty to the third generation. And different marks are printed on them according to their future value. And this money is made in the city of Cambaluc by those who are deputed for this by the king, & not by others. And each year he has so great quantity and supply of them made in the city of Cambaluc that he would pay with it for all the treasure of the world, though it costs him nothing. And in almost all the kingdoms subject to his rule none is allowed to make or spend any other money. And when these sheets are made in the way that I have told you, he has all the payments made with them, and has them distributed to each one through all the provinces and kingdoms & through all his cities and lands where he has rule, & even lands which do not obey him which do not spend this money; and none dare refuse them on pain of losing his life immediately; and no one from other kingdoms can spend other money within the lands of the great Kaan. Moreover I tell you that all the people and regions of men who are under his rule very gladly take these sheets in payment, because wherever they go under the rule of the great Kaan they take them and make all their payments with them both for goods and for pearls and for precious stones and for gold and for silver and for all other things which they carry and sell or buy, of however great value; they can buy everything with them, and they make payment with the sheets of which I have told you as if they were altogether of real gold or silver. Moreover I tell you that they are so light that the sheet which is put for ten bezants of gold weighs not one. Moreover I tell you that many times a year the merchants come many together from Indie or from other parts with pearls and with precious stones and with gold and with silver and with other things, these are cloth of gold and of silk; and these merchants give all of these things to none in this city but to the great lord. And the great lord calls twelve wise men who are chosen [to be] over those things and who are very clever in doing this; and he commands them to look very carefully at those things which the merchants have brought and to have them paid with what it seems to them that they are worth. And those twelve wise men look at those things and when they have valued them according to their knowledge they have them paid immediately with interest that which it seems to them that they are worth, with those sheets of which I have told you. And the merchants take them very gladly because they know well that they would not have so much from any other, and secondly because they are paid for them at once, and also because they change them afterwards, as has been said, for all the things which they buy both there and through all the lands of the great lord; and also it is lighter than anything else to carry by road. And if they are from some place where these note are not used, they invest them in other merchandise good for their countries. Moreover I tell you without any mistake that many times a year the merchants bring so many things that they are well worth 400000 bezants of gold and the great lord buys of them each year so much that it is without end, and he has them all paid with those sheets, a thing which costs him little or nothing, as you have heard. And again I tell you that many times a year an order goes through the town of Cambaluc that all those who have precious stones and pearls and gold and silver or any other dear things must bring them to the mint of the great lord, & he will have them well and liberally paid with that money according to the proper value. And they do it and bring them there very willingly, because they would not receive so much for them from any other, in so great abundance that it is without number, and all are paid with sheets without delay or loss to them. And he who should not wish to bring them, stays at home. And in this way the great lord has all the gold and the silver and the pearls and the precious stones of all his lands. And again I tell you another thing which does well to say. For when one has kept these sheets so long that they are torn and are spoilt through too great age, though they are very durable, then he takes them to the mint of the great lord and they are changed for new and clean ones, so, indeed, that he leaves three in a hundred of them for the stamp. And again I shall tell you a pretty fact which does well to tell in our book. For if a baron or other man whoever he might be wishes to buy gold or silver or precious stones or pearls to make his vessels or his girdles or his other work, he goes off to the mint of the great lord and carries some of those sheets and gives them in payment for the gold and for the silver which he buys from the master of the mint. And never is gold or silver spent, but all his armies and officials come to be paid with this sort of money of paper (of which he has as much made as he pleases), of which the value is the same to them as if it were of gold or of silver; and everything necessary for the court is bought. Now I have told you the way and the reason why the great lord must have and has more treasure than any man of this world, and you have well heard how and in what manner; & it costs him nothing, so that he can well spend marvellous sums. And everyone is obliged to buy those moneys from him. Moreover I will tell you a greater thing, that all the lords of the earth have not so great riches, treasures, and expenses as the great lord has alone. Now I have told you and described all the facts how the great lord makes money of sheets.

* * *

Here he tells of the wine which the people of the Kaan drink. And again you may know that the greater part of the people of the province of Catai drink good wine, and it is such a wine as I shall describe to you. For instead of wine they make a drink of rice, and they make the rice boil with very many other good spices mixed together, and they make it—the drink or wine—in such a way and so well and with such a flavour that it is better worth drinking than any other wine of grapes, and men could not wish better. And it is very clear and sparkling & very fragrant and beautiful. And it makes a man become drunken sooner than any other wine because it is very hot stuff, and it is sweet.

* * *

[For] Master Marc Pol was in this city many times and determined with great diligence to notice and understand all the conditions of the place, describing them in his notes, as will be briefly here said below. It was contained in that writing first of all that the city of Quinsai is so large that in circuit it is in the common belief a hundred miles round or thereabout, because the streets and canals in it are very wide and large. Then there are squares where they hold market, which on account of the vast multitudes which meet in them are necessarily very large and spacious. And it is placed in this way, that it has on one side a lake of fresh water which is very clear, and on the other there is an enormous river which, entering by many great and small canals which run in every part of the city, both takes away all impurities and then enters the said lake, and from that runs to the Ocean. And this makes the air very wholesome; and one can go all about the city by land and by these streams. And the streets and canals are wide and great so that boats are able to travel there conveniently and carts to carry the things necessary for the inhabitants. And there is a story that it has 12000 bridges, between great and small, for the greater part of stone—for some are built of wood. And for each of these bridges, or for the greater part, a great & large ship could easily pass under the arch of it; and for the others smaller ships could pass. But those which are made over the principal canals and the chief streets are arched so high and with such skill that a boat can pass under them without a mast, and yet there pass over them carriages and horses, so well are the streets inclined to fit the height. And let no one be surprised if there are so many bridges, because I tell you that this town is all situated in water of lagoons as Venese is, and is also all surrounded by water, and so it is needful that there may be so many bridges for this, that people may be able to go through all the town both inside and out by land; and if they were not in such numbers you could not go from one place to the other by land, but only by boats. On the other side of the city there is a ditch perhaps forty miles long which shuts it in on that side, and is very wide and full of water which comes from the said river. And this was made by order of those ancient kings of that province so as to be able to draw off the river into it every time that it rose above the banks; and it serves also as a defence for the city, and the earth which was dug out was put on the inner side, which makes the likeness of a little hill which surrounds it. There are ten principal open spaces, beside infinite others for the districts, which are square, that is half a mile for a side. And along the front of those there is a main street forty paces wide, which runs straight from one end of the city to the other with many bridges which cross it level and conveniently; and every four miles is found one of these squares such as have two miles (as has been said) of circuit. There is in the same way a very broad canal which runs parallel to the said street at the back of the said squares, and on the near bank of this there are built great houses of stone where all the merchants who come from Indie and from other parts deposit their goods & merchandise that they may be near and handy to the squares. And on each of the said squares three days a week there is a concourse of from forty to fifty thousand persons who come to market and bring everything you can desire for food, because there is always a great supply of victuals; of game, that is to say of roebuck, red-deer, fallow-deer, hares, rabbits, and of birds, partridges, pheasants, francolins, quails, fowls, capons, and so many ducks and geese that more could not be told; for they rear so many of them in that lake that for one Venetian silver groat may be had a pair of geese and two pair of ducks. There are too the shambles where they slaughter the large animals like calves, oxen, kids, and lambs, the which flesh the rich men and great lords eat. But the rest who are of low position do not abstain from all the other kinds of unclean flesh, without any respect. There are always on the said squares all sorts of vegetables and fruits, and above all the rest immense pears, which weigh ten pounds a piece, which are white inside like a paste, and very fragrant; peaches in their seasons, yellow and white, very delicate. Grapes nor wine do not grow there, but very good dried ones are brought from elsewhere, and likewise wine, of which the inhabitants do not make too much count, being used to that of rice and spices. Then there comes every day, brought from the Ocean sea up the river for the space of twenty-five miles, great quantity of fish; and there is also a supply of that from the lake (for there are always fishermen who do nothing else), which is of different sorts according to the seasons of the year, and because of the impurities which come from the city it is fat and savoury. Whoever saw the quantity of the said fish would never think that it could be sold, and yet in a few hours it has all been taken away, so great is the multitude of the inhabitants who are used to live delicately; for they eat both fish and flesh at the same meal. All the said ten squares are surrounded by high houses, and underneath are shops where they work at all sorts of trades, and sell all sorts of merchandise, and spicery, jewels, pearls; and in some shops nothing else is sold but wine made of rice with spices, for they continually go making it fresh and fresh, and it is cheap. In other streets are stationed the courtesans, who are in so great number that I dare not say it; and not only near the squares, where places are usually assigned to them, but all over the city. And they stay very sumptuously with great perfumes and with many maid-servants, & the houses all decorated. These women are very clever and practised in knowing how to flatter and coax with ready words and suited to each kind of person, so that the foreigners who have once indulged themselves with them stay as it were in an ecstasy, and are so much taken with their sweetness and charms that they can never forget them. And from this it comes to pass that when they return home they say that they have been in Quinsai, that is in the city of Heaven, and never see the hour that they may be able to go back there again. In other streets are stationed all the physicians, astrologers, who also teach to read and to write. And infinite other trades have their places round about the said squares; on each of which there are two great palaces, one at one end and the other at the other, where are stationed the lords deputed by the king, who make inquiry immediately if any difference occurs between the merchants, and in the same way between any of the inhabitants of those quarters. The said lords are charged to watch every day whether the guards who are set on the neighbouring bridges (as will be said below) are actually there or have failed, and punish them as they think right.

Along the principal street of which we have spoken, which runs from one end of the city to the other, there are on one side and on the other houses, very large palaces with their gardens, and near by them houses of artisans who work in their shops; and at all hours are met people who are going up and down on their business, so that to see so great a crowd anyone would believe that it would not be possible that victuals are found enough to be able to feed it; and yet on every market day all the said squares are covered and filled with people and merchants who bring them both on carts and on boats, and all is disposed of. And again it was contained there in the said writing that this city had twelve different manner of trades, one of each craft, which are reckoned the more important and have greater dealings than the others, for there are very many others. And each trade of these twelve has 12000 stations, that is to say 12000 houses for each trade of the aforesaid. And in each house or station there were at least ten men to exercise those arts, and some fifteen, and some twenty, and thirty, and some forty. And do not understand that they are all masters, but men who do what the masters and patrons order them. And all this is necessary because many other cities of the province are supplied with necessaries from this city.

* * *

And again there were many abbeys in that place round the lake and many monasteries of idols, which are in the very greatest numbers, where stay a large number of monks who serve them. And again I tell you that in the middle of the lake are two little islands on which there are, on each one, very wonderful palaces very great and noble and rich, so well made and so ornamented that they are really like some emperors palaces, with so many rooms and galleries that it could not be believed. And so when some notable one wishes to make a great wedding or any great banquet in a smart place they go to one of these palaces and there with dignity can make their wedding and their feast. And they find there all the furniture that is needed for the banquet, that is of plate and of linen and of dishes and everything else which they need according to their usages, which are all kept in the said palaces for the people of the said city for this purpose, because they were built by them. And sometimes there would be a hundred, and some would wish to make feasts and others weddings, and yet all would be accommodated in different rooms and verandahs with such order that one does not inconvenience the others. Besides this, boats or barges are found on the said lake in great numbers, large and small, to go for enjoyment and to give oneself pleasure; and in these there can stay, ten, fifteen, and twenty, and more persons, because they are fifteen to twenty paces long with broad and flat bottoms, so that they sail without rocking on either side. And every one who likes to enjoy himself with women or with his companions takes one of the boats like these, which are always kept adorned with beautiful seats and tables and with all the other furniture necessary for making a feast. Above they are covered and flat, where men stand with poles which they stick into the ground (for the said lake is not more than two paces deep) and guide the said barges where they are ordered. The covering on the inside part is painted with different colours and patterns, and likewise all the barge; and there are windows round about which they can shut and open, so that those who stay seated at the meal at the sides may be able to look this way and that and delight the eyes with the variety and beauty of the places to which they are taken. Here come the best wines, hence are brought perfect confections; and in this way those men go about this lake rejoicing together, for their mind and care is set on nothing else but bodily pleasure and enjoyment in feasting together. And you shall know that this lake gives them greater refreshment and comfort than anything else which may be had on land, because on one side it lies along the city so that all the grandeur and beauty of that is seen from afar while one stays on the said barges, so many are the palaces, temples, monasteries, gardens with very lofty trees, set upon the waterside. And barges like these are found on the said lake at all times with people who go for enjoyment; for the inhabitants of this city never think of anything else but after that they have done their work or business to spend part of the day with their ladies.

* * *

And first you may know quite truly that all the ways and streets in all this town of Quinsai are well paved with good hewn stones and with baked bricks, so that the whole city is very clean; and so are all the chief ways and streets and the causeways of all the province of Mangi paved so that one can ride at any time conveniently there wherever one wishes quite cleanly both on horseback and on foot through all the lands of it without soiling the feet. For the land is very low and flat and there is very deep [mud] when it rains, so that if it were not that the ways are all paved (i.e. where it is needed) one sometimes could not ride there nor go, on foot or on horse. But because the couriers of the great Kaan could not travel quickly with horses over paved streets, therefore a part of the street at the side is left without pavement for the sake of the said couriers. In truth the main street of which we have spoken above, which runs from one end of the city to the other, is paved like this with stones and with bricks ten paces along either side, but in the middle it is all filled with a small and fine gravel, with its vaulted conduits which lead the rain waters into the canals near by, so that it always stays dry. Now on this street are always seen going up and down certain long carriages covered and furnished with hangings and cushions of silk, in which six persons can stay. And they are taken every day by men and women who wish to go for pleasure. And an endless number of these carriages are seen at all times going along the said street, down the middle of it; and they go to gardens where they are received by the gardeners under certain shades made for this purpose, and there they stay to give themselves a good time all day with their ladies, and then in the evening they go home again in the said carriages. And in this city are quite 10000 very fine and great streets. And again I tell you that in this town of Quinsai are quite three thousand artificial baths, which spring from the ground, these are stoves, where the men and the women bathe and take them great delight and go there several times a month; for they live very cleanly in their bodies. Moreover I tell you that they are the most beautiful baths and the best and the largest that are in the world. For I tell you that they are so large that more than a hundred men or a hundred women can well bathe themselves there at one time.

Marco Polo, *The Description of the World*, translated by A. C. Moule and Paul Pelliot. (London: George Routledge & Sons, 2 vols., 1938), 185–87, 249–50, 327–28.

DISCUSSION QUESTIONS

1. Why did Khubilai Khan build such a splendid palace at Shangdu simply for hunting? Why is hunting so significant for the Mongols?
2. Judging from Marco's description and your own additional reading about European cities during this time, how would his native city of Venice compare with Hangzhou (known to him as Quinsai)?
3. Judging from his own background, why would Marco be fascinated by paper money?
4. Why would Europeans originally not believe Marco's descriptions?

Anonymous, Portrait of Khubilai Khan

The portrait of Khubilai derives from around 1260, the time he acceded to the position of Great Khan. One distinguished art historian, based on a study of the portrait and a depiction of Khubilai's wife, Chabi, in another painting, has identified Aniko, a Nepalese artist at the court of the Great Khan, as the painter, but this attribution remains controversial.

Anonymous, "Portrait of Khubilai Khan," ca. 1260. National Palace Museum, Taipei.

Liu Guandao, Khubilai Khan on a Hunt

Around 1280, the Chinese artist Liu Guandao received an imperial commission to paint Khubilai on a hunt. By that time, Khubilai had developed an appreciation of Chinese painting and had acquired paintings for the Chinese Imperial Collection of Paintings. Vanity played a role in the commission of this painting, but affirmation of a Mongol pastime may also have been a factor.

Liu Guandao "Khubilai Khan on a Hunt," ca. 1280. National Palace Museum, Taipei, Taiwan.

DISCUSSION QUESTIONS

1. Describe Khubilai's clothing and appearance in each of these paintings. What do your descriptions reveal? What is the significance of such revelations in an analysis of Khubilai's rule over China?
2. Why would Khubilai choose to have himself depicted on a hunt? What does that tell us regarding his governance of China?

Yuanshi

The Yuanshi *is one of the twenty-five dynastic histories of China, each of which was sponsored by the court. Because the succeeding dynasty compiled the history of its predecessor, the* Yuanshi *was completed in the late fourteenth century during the Ming dynasty (1368–1644). Like all dynastic histories, the* Yuanshi *consists of four sections: annals, or a year-by-year account of court actions; lists of holders of important official positions; essays on the military, the tax systems, and other subjects of interest to the court; and biographies of leading figures. One of the sometimes stereotyped biographies is of Khubilai Khan's wife, Chabi. This biography, which is actually a sketch, reveals the attitudes and values the court wished to convey.*

Chabi had given cloth to each member of the Imperial Household. Khubilai said: "This is needed by the military. Why are you giving it away?" From that time on, Chabi organized the palace ladies to take old bow string, make it into thread, and turn it into clothing. Its pliability and denseness were greater than that of damask.

Khubilai brought the treasures of the Song [dynasty] to the palace and summoned Chabi to look at them. She looked at them and then left. Khubilai sent a eunuch to ask which of the treasures she wanted. She responded: "Song saved these objects to bequeath to their sons and grandsons. The sons and grandsons could not protect them, and they came to us. How could I bear to take even one thing?"

Song Lian, et al., *Yuanshi,* translated by Morris Rossabi (Beijing: Zhonghua shuju, 1976), 2870–71.

DISCUSSION QUESTIONS

1. In questioning Chabi's use of cloth, what kind of values is Khubilai reaffirming?
2. How does Khubilai's abstemiousness jibe with Marco Polo's description of the elaborate palaces at Shangdu?

Chŏng In-ji, Koryŏ sa

The Koryŏ sa *is the official history of the Korean Koryŏ dynasty (918–1392), compiled by Chŏng In-ji between 1445 and 1451. It resembled the* Yuanshi *because it was court-sponsored and written by the succeeding dynasty. Also like the* Yuanshi, *it presented the court's viewpoints on events. The court conveyed the images it wanted. In this case, it transmitted the values and image that Khubilai Khan wished to purvey.*

A Korean envoy named Cho offered Khubilai a beautiful vase, and the Great Khan's response was:

"Painting gold on porcelain—is that to make the porcelain strong?"

Cho's answer was: "No, it is only to decorate the vase."

The Khan then asked: "Can the gold be used again?"

Cho replied: "Porcelain breaks so easily, so also naturally gold. How can it be used again?"

Khubilai Khan then said: "From now on do not use gold and do not present it to me."

Chŏng In-ji, *Koryŏ sa* (Tokyo, 1909); adapted by Morris Rossabi from Kim Chewon, "Random Notes on Literary References to Koryŏ Ceramics," *Far Eastern Ceramic Bulletin* 9.3–4 (Sept.–Dec. 1957): 30–34.

DISCUSSION QUESTIONS

1. Explain Khubilai's reaction to this present.
2. In Khubilai's view, what might happen to the Mongols if they accept such presents?

'Phags-pa lama, Prince Jin-gim's Textbook of Tibetan Buddhism

*The 'Phags-pa lama (1235–1280), a Tibetan monk of the Sa-skya sect, had his life changed with the arrival of the Mongols. Invited by Khubilai Khan to travel to his court in China in the mid-1250s, 'Phags-pa began a relationship of two decades with the Mongol ruler and his family. Chabi, Khubilai's most prominent wife, was impressed with the Tibetan monk, who instructed her about Tibetan Buddhism's precepts and practices. In 1258, Khubilai, perhaps influenced by his wife, invited 'Phags-pa to participate in a Buddhist-Daoist debate that was designed to end the sometimes violent conflicts between the two religions. Thanks in part to 'Phags-pa's skills as a debater and an interrogator, the Buddhists emerged victorious. Khubilai then named 'Phags-pa a state preceptor (*guoshi*) in 1260, administrator of Tibet and of government relations with Buddists in China, and an imperial preceptor (*dishi*) in 1270. In turn, 'Phags-pa rewarded his benefactor by proclaiming Khubilai to be an incarnate of Manjusri, the Boddhisattva of Wisdom in the Buddhist pantheon, and by recruiting Aniko (1244–1306), a talented artist and craftsman who planned and constructed notable buildings in Daidu (Beijing) and may have painted the official images of Khubilai and Chabi. In the 1270s, 'Phags-pa returned to Tibet, where he shared power with a civilian administrator, an untenable arrangement that may have led to his death. Monks from the Sa-skya sect accused the civilian administrator of poisoning 'Phags-pa, and within a year of his death, the civilian administrator had been executed.*

'Phags-pa's close relationship with both Khubilai and Chabi prompted them to assign him to tutor their son and Khubilai's chosen successor, Jingim, particularly on Buddhist principles. As an instructional aid for his student, 'Phags-pa wrote the Ses-bya rab-gsal (What One Should Know) *and then began to refer to him as "Boddhisattva Imperial Prince." The work provided a simple explication of Buddhist precepts as well as a brief geneology of Jingim's Mongol ancestors.*

Three thousand two hundred and fifty years after the Buddha's Nirvana, Jiṅ-gir (Genghis) became King up North in Hor (Mongolia); he enjoyed the fruit of his merit which had been stored up in former lives.

Beginning from the North he brought many countries of different languages and races under his power, and by his strength he became like a 'Khor-los sgyur-ba'i King. His son Mo-go-ta (=Ögödäi), widely known as Ga-gan (mong. Qagan=Khan) succeeded him and the dominions became even more extensive than before.

His son was Go-yug-gan (=Güyük Khan); he also ruled as King (=Khan) over the realm.

Genghis' younger son was Do-lo (Tolui); he also obtained the rank of Khan and ruled supreme.

His eldest son was called Mon-go (Möngkä); he as well obtained the highest rank and ruled supreme.

His younger brother is known as Go-pe-la (Qubilai). He too was appointed Khan and ruled over far more dominions than his predecessors and, after entering the Door of the Precious Teaching, he has protected his realm according to the Dharma, and also manifested the Teacher's Teaching.

His eldest son is Jin-gim, who is endowed with all the glory of Heaven and who is also resplendent with the Ornament of the Precious Dharma. His brothers are Mangala, Nomogan and others. Each one is provided with his own virtues and riches and has his own sons and lineage.

So I have told [the history], beginning with the Sa-kya royal lineage up to the Imperial dynasty of our own time.

And so Man-pos bkur-ba was appointed as the first King. At that time the sentient beings mutually took from each other's fields what had not been given. When they were questioned by the King's men they even lied that they had not taken it. Because they were put to death by the King's men, many bad (mi-dge-ba, akusala) deeds, killing and so on, were committed; then the sentient beings who did these deeds died, transferred consciousness ('si-'phos) and were born among the Animals; after that they were born among the Hungry Ghosts. Then they were born successively in the Hells. When beings were born for the first time where they had not been before, in mNar-med-pa [the lowest Hell], then the Origination of the world was completed. In this way man's life became gradually shorter because they had committed negative deeds, and their objects for enjoyment dwindled; the life of the people of Dzambu'i glin became 80.000 years long and those Hell-beings who had been newly born in mNar-med had the same [length of] life.

So the origination of the World of Sentient Beings takes nineteen Medium Aeons; the origin of the Inanimate World takes one Medium Aeon, and thus the Origination takes twenty Medium Aeons.

When people's age in Dzambu'i glin was 80.000 the Continuance (gnas-pa'i, sthiti) Aeon began; this world continues for twenty Medium Aeons. When their life is 10 years the Weapon Aeon (mTshon-gyi bskal-pa [bar-ma], Sastrantara-kalpa) comes, which lasts seven days; then the Sickness Medium Aeon (Nadkyi bskal-pa bar-ma, Rogantara-kalpa) of seven days and seven months, and then the Famine Aeon (Mu-ge'i bskal-pa bar-ma, Durbhiksantara-kalpa) of seven days, seven months and seven years, and because of that man has [then] almost disappeared.

When the remaining ones catch sight of one another, they love one another and live in harmony, because there are very few left; by the performance of positive (dge-ba, kusala) deeds (desisting from killing etc.) their life and objects for enjoyment gradually increase until their life is again 80.000 years. While it is increasing the 'Khor-los sgyur-ba Kings appear; they protect the sentient beings by the Law of the Dharma (chos-khrims, dharmasastra). In times of decrease the Perfect Buddhas (rDzogs-pa'i sans-rgyas, Saṃbuddha) appear in the world; they are the Saviours ('dren-pa) of the sentient beings.

The Solitary Buddhas (Ran sans-rgyas, Pratyeka-buddha) appear in times of increase as well as decrease; they form a Field of Merit for the sentient beings.

After the duration of twenty Medium Aeons the Destruction ('jig-pa, vibhava) begins. The World of Sentient beings is the first which it destroys. So new births in mNar-med are cut off and when the birth of beings there is finished, and if their Karma is also exhausted after their death, they are born into other destinies ('gro-ba, gati); those with whom it is not so go to the Hells above, or they will be born into hells in other World Spheres.

Thus, when mNar-med-pa has become empty and the hells above it also, they will be born among the Hungry Ghosts. In the same way the Hungry Ghosts and the Animals will also become empty.

Those humans who live in the Northern Continent (Byan-gi sGra-mi-snan, Uttara-kuru), are an exception. For the 'Dod-pa Gods [it is the rule that] they are born in the Absorption which they have acquired by their True Nature (chos-nid, dharmata), and they will be born in the First Absorption (bsam-gtan, dhyana). The beings of the Northern Continent are born among the 'Dod-pa Gods; there they acquire the Thought of the First Absorption, and they will be born there. Those in the First Absorption have, even so by their True Nature, acquired the Second Absorption; when this has been born in their mindstream (rgyud, samtana) they are born, after death and transference, in the Second Absorption. In this way [everything] from the Lowest Hell to the Tshans-pa World becomes empty, and this goes on (thogs) for nineteen Medium Aeons. Then seven suns will rise in the Four Continents. There falls no rain, and the first sun desiccates the orchards of fruit trees which grow from water. The second one dries up ponds and small rivers; the third sun does the same with the Four Big Rivers, even the Ganges etc; the fourth one makes even Lake Ma-dros-pa (Anavatapta) fall dry; the fifth sun desiccates the Outer Ocean until it is knee-high only, the sixth sun dries up even the rest of the Outer Ocean, and the seventh one makes this our world go up in one sheet of flame. From the lowest Hell to the Tshans-pa World [everything] is destroyed by fire.

In this way the destruction of the world goes on for (thogs) one Medium Aeon.

Then there is an Empty Aeon. That is empty, also for twenty Medium Aeons. So there are eighty Medium Aeons in the Origination-, Continuance-, Destruction-, and Empty Aeons. Together these are called a Great Aeon. Hence it is the same as the life of the Tshans-ris Gods and so forth.

The destruction of the Inanimate World is effected by fire as well as by water and wind. The destruction by fire is as has been explained above just now. After the Origination has again happened successively seven times, the Origination World is destroyed by water, and this wipes out [everything] up to the Second Absorption. In the 'Od gsal Abode a big mass of clouds accumulates, and then, after torrents of rain have fallen, the Inanimate World has disappeared, like salt which dissolves in water, and then even the water itself dries up. In this way, after it has been annihilated by water, it will be destroyed again seven times by fire, just like before.

Then it is again wiped out by water; and so, after every seven destructions by fire there is destruction by water; after the seventh destruction by water there come again seven destructions by fire. After that the Origination World is annihilated by wind and this destroys [everything] up to the Third Absorption, and so, when the storm shatters even the King of Mountains, Ri-rab, of course all other mountains are destroyed and shattered by the wind.

The Fourth Absorption cannot be destroyed by an outside cause, but when the beings are born there, they are born together with a heavenly palace, and when they die, they are destroyed together with the palace.

End of the description of the Inanimate World, the Sentient Beings in the Animate World, their Origination and Destruction.

Prince Jin-gim's Textbook of Tibetan Buddhism, translated by Constance Hoog (Leiden: E. J. Brill, 1983), 42–46.

DISCUSSION QUESTIONS

1. Why did Khubilai have his son and chosen successor Jingim receive instruction on Buddhism by the most prominent Tibetan Buddhist at his court? What does this reveal about Khubilai's attitudes toward education and governance?
2. What does such religious instruction for the Crown Prince disclose about Khubilai's and the Mongols' attitudes toward the sacred and the profane?

Francesco Balducci Pegolotti, Cathay and the Way Thither

Francesco Balducci Pegolotti (ca. 1280–after 1347) was a merchant in fourteenth-century Florence who worked for a number of companies and local governments. Fragmentary records indicate that he conducted business in London, Antwerp, and Cyprus, among other places, during his peripatetic commercial career. In Cyprus and Armenia, he negotiated better terms of trade for all Florentine merchants.

His commercial handbook offers precise and precious information about the prices and products found along the Silk Roads. He never traveled far toward the

East and must have received most of his data from merchants who had. His descriptions of the routes from the Middle East to China and from Turkey to the Il-Khanate capital at Tabriz were remarkably accurate, even to the distances and the number of days required for the voyages. He also specified the number of men needed for long-distance caravans and the imports and exports from specific regions en route and offered useful information on foreign languages and business customs. More helpful still were his descriptions of the values of coins and different weights and measures and even the differing lengths of cloth and the quality of gold and silver throughout the oases and other stopping places. The range of his information was truly remarkable.

The road you travel from Tana to Cathay is perfectly safe, whether by day or by night, according to what the merchants say who have used it. Only if the merchant, in going or coming, should die upon the road, everything belonging to him will become the perquisite of the lord of the country in which he dies, and the officers of the lord will take possession of all. And in like manner if he die in Cathay. But if his brother be with him, or an intimate friend and comrade calling himself his brother, then to such an one they will surrender the property of the deceased, and so it will be rescued.

And there is another danger: this is when the lord of the country dies, and before the new lord who is to have the lordship is proclaimed; during such intervals there have sometimes been irregularities practised on the Franks, and other foreigners. (They call *Franks* all the Christians of these parts from Romania westward.) And neither will the roads be safe to travel until the other lord be proclaimed who is to reign in room of him who is deceased.

Cathay is a province which contained a multitude of cities and towns. Among others there is one in particular, that is to say the capital city, to which is great resort of merchants, and in which there is a vast amount of trade; and this city is called Cambalec. And the said city hath a circuit of one hundred miles, and is all full of people and houses and of dwellers in the said city.

You may calculate that a merchant with a dragoman, and with two men servants, and with goods to the value of twenty-five thousand golden florins, should spend on his way to Cathay from sixty to eighty *sommi* of silver, and not more if he manage well; and for all the road back again from Cathay to Tana, including the expenses of living and the pay of servants, and all other charges, the cost will be about five *sommi* per head of pack animals, or something less. And you may reckon the *sommo* to be worth five golden florins. You may reckon also that each ox-waggon will require one ox, and will carry ten cantars Genoese weight; and the camel-waggon will require three camels, and will carry thirty cantars Genoese weight; and the horse-waggon will require one horse, and will commonly carry six and half cantars of silk, at 250 Genoese pounds to the cantar. And a bale of silk may be reckoned at between 110 and 115 Genoese pounds.

You may reckon also that from Tana to Sara the road is less safe than on any other part of the journey; and yet even when this part of the road is at its worst, if you are some sixty men in the company you will go as safely as if you were in your own house.

Anyone from Genoa or from Venice, wishing to go to the places above-named, and to make the journey to Cathay, should carry linens with him, and if he visit Organci he will dispose of these well. In Organci he should purchase *sommi* of silver, and with these he should proceed without making any further investment, unless it be some bales of the very finest stuffs which go in small bulk, and cost no more for carriage than coarser stuffs would do.

Merchants who travel this road can ride on horseback or on asses, or mounted in any way that they list to be mounted.

Whatever silver the merchants may carry with them as far as Cathay the lord of Cathay will take from them and put into his treasury. And to merchants who thus bring silver they give that paper money of theirs in exchange. This is of yellow paper, stamped with the seal of the lord aforesaid. And this money is called *balishi*; and with this money you can readily buy silk and all other merchandize that you have a desire to buy. And all the people of the country are bound to receive it. And yet you shall not pay a higher price for your goods because your money is of paper. And of the said paper money there are three kinds, one being worth more than another, according to the value which has been established for each by that lord.

And you may reckon that you can buy for one *sommo* of silver nineteen or twenty pounds of Cathay silk, when reduced to Genoese weight, and that the *sommo* should weigh eight and a half ounces of Genoa, and should be of the alloy of eleven ounces and seventeen deniers to the pound.

You may reckon also that in Cathay you should get three or three and a half pieces of damasked silk for a *sommo*; and from three and a half to five pieces of *nacchetti* of silk and gold, likewise for a *sommo* of silver.

Comparison of the weights and measures of Cathay and of Tana

				lbs.	ozs.
The maund of	Sara = in	Genoa	weight	6	2
"	Organci	"	"	3	9
"	Oltrarre	"	"	3	9
"	Armalec	"	"	2	8
"	Camexu	"	"	2	0

Tana on the Black Sea

At Tana, as shall next be shown, they use a variety of weights and measures, viz.:

The *cantar*, which is that of Genoa.
The *great pound* = 20 lbs. Genoese.
The *ruotolo*, of which 20 = 1 great pound.
The *little pound*, which is the Genoese pound.
The *tocchetto*, of which 12 = 1 great pound.
The *saggio* of which 45 = 1 sommo.
The *picco*.

Wax, ladanum, iron, tin, copper, pepper, ginger, all coarser spices, cotton, madder, and suet, cheese, flax, and oil, honey, and the like, sell by the great pound.

Silk, saffron, amber wrought in rosaries and the like, and all small spices sell by the little pound.

Vair-skins by the 1000; and 1020 go to the 1000.

Ermines by the 1000; 1000 to the 1000.

Foxes, sables, fitches and martens, wolfskins, deerskins, and all cloths of silk or gold, by the piece.

Common stuffs, and canvasses of every kind sell by the *picco*.

Tails are sold by the bundle at twenty to the bundle.

Oxhides by the hundred in tale, giving a hundred and no more.

Horse and pony hides by the piece.

Gold and pearls are sold by the *saggio*. Wheat and all other corn and pulse is sold at Tana by a measure which they call *cascito*. Greek wine and all Latin wines are sold by the cask as they come. Malmsey and wines of Triglia and Candia are sold by the measure.

Caviar is sold by the *fusco*, and a *fusco* is the tail-half of the fish's skin, full of fish's roe.

Henry Yule, *Cathay and the Way Thither*, new ed. by Henri Cordier (London: Hakluyt Society, 1913–16), 152–58.

DISCUSSION QUESTIONS

1. What part of Pegolotti's instructions would offer confidence to long-distance travelers, particularly merchants?
2. Pegolotti never traveled to Central and East Asia. What do the details he provides reveal about East-West contacts during this era?
3. Why was silk such an optimal item in long-distance trade?
4. What kinds of products were ideal for long-distance trade?

Marco Polo, The Description of the World

Marco Polo may have viewed his reminiscences as aids for future travelers to China. He offers vignettes about the oases and towns along the Silk Roads, emphasizing that the inhabitants were often extremely hospitable. In the case of Camul (modern Hami), they even lent their wives to weary travelers.

See the headnote on p. 101 for additional information on this text.

Here he tells of the province of Camul. Camul is a province which used to be a kingdom by itself, in the great province of Tangut. There are towns and villages enough under it, and the chief town is called Camul like the province. And the province is towards the plough-beam between two deserts, for on the one side is the very great desert of Lop of which we have spoken above and on the other is a little desert of three days march in length. And the people of that province are all idolaters like the others narrated above, and have a language for themselves. And they live on the fruit of the land; for they have things to eat and to drink enough, both for themselves and they give and sell them to the wayfarers who pass that way, to whom they will and as they please, and to merchants who carry them to other places. And they are men of very cheerful looks and all greatly given to amusement, for they are devoted to nothing else but the playing of instruments and singing and dancing and briefly in taking great bodily enjoyment. They delight also in reading and writing after their manner. And I tell you that, led astray from of old by their idols, these people have such a custom. If a stranger passes through the region and comes to him to his house to lodge, he is too much delighted at it, and receives him with great joy, and labours to do everything to please. And he tells his wife, daughters, sisters, and other relations to do all that the stranger wishes more than for him; and he leaves his house and his wife for the stranger, and goes immediately to do his work and stays two days or three on the farm or elsewhere, where he will. And from there they send all that their guests need (none the less with payment for them); nor do they ever return home while the stranger stays there. And the stranger stays with his wife in the house and does as he likes and lies with her in a bed just as if she were his wife, and they continue in great enjoyment. And in this way it can be said that all those of this city and province aforesaid of Camul are shamed by their wives as you have heard. But I tell you that they do not hold it as a shame to them but regard this as great honour and glory, because of the general custom which is in all that province; and very pleasing to their idols when they give so good a reception to wayfarers in need of rest, and that for this reason all their goods, children, and wealth are multiplied and kept from all dangers, and all things succeed for them with the greatest happiness. And the women are very fair and gay and very wanton and most obedient to all that their husbands order, and greatly enjoy this custom. Now it happened one day that at the time when Mongu the great Kaan, fifth general lord of all the

Tartars, reigned and was their lord in this province, then it was reported to him how those of this province of Camul so made their wives commit adultery with strangers, and he loathed such a custom. And that Mongu, having learnt the habits and so shameful customs, sends to them immediately commanding under very great penalties that they and all of that province must for the future leave this so indecent belief [and] not dare to lodge the strangers any more in that way; but preserving the honour of their wives should provide the wayfarers with public lodgings; & that they do not maintain any more that shaming of their wives. And when they of Camul had had this order they were much grieved by it, and sadly obeyed the commandments of the king for about three years; and then in the end, seeing that their lands were not yielding the accustomed fruits and that in their houses many misfortunes followed one another, they were in counsel how to remedy so great a loss and counsel and do that which I shall tell you. For they sent their ambassadors who took a great & beautiful present and carry it to Mongu and pray him that so great a wrong with so great loss to them & danger should not be done, & that he would be content that they might observe that which by their old fathers and grandfathers had been left them with such solemnity [and] would leave them to make the use of their wives which their ancestors had left them, and that otherwise they knew not how to live, and could not; and they tell him how their ancestors had said that for the pleasure which they made for the strangers with their wives and with their things that their idols held them in great favour and that their corn and their labour on the land multiplied greatly because of it; for since they failed to do these pleasures & kindnesses to the strangers their houses went from bad to worse & to ruin. And when the ambassadors, furnished with their great & most notable gifts, were come to the lands of the great Kaan they were joyfully received, as is the custom with those who come with their hands full (I do not speak of the rulers of these our parts, for they are far removed from this opinion), & when the great Kaan had heard their embassy he laboured to remove this contemptible belief from their minds, but they remained ever more sure that they could not hope for any good from their gods when they felt displeasure & if they dared to do contrary to their laudable commandments. And when Mongu Kaan heard it he says, For my part I have done my duty; but since you wish your shame and contempt so much, then you may have it. Go and live according to your customs, and make your wives a charitable gift to travellers. And then he revoked the order which he had made about this and consents that they do their will with their evil usage. And I tell you that with this answer they went home with the greatest joy of the whole people and from that time till now they have always kept up and still keep up that custom throughout that province.

Marco Polo, *The Description of the World*, translated by A. C. Moule and Paul Pelliot (London: George Routledge & Sons, 2 vols., 1938), 154–55.

DISCUSSION QUESTION

1. How would Marco's description of "Camul" (or Hami) provide comfort to merchants and others traveling across Eurasia?

Zhou Daguan, A Record of Cambodia

Temür (r. 1294–1307), Khubilai Khan's grandson and successor, dispatched Zhou Daguan (ca. 1270–ca. 1350) as an envoy to Angkor, ostensibly to announce the enthronement of a new emperor in China. Little is known about Zhou except that he was a native of the area around Wenzhou, a commercial center along China's southeast coast. More than likely, the emperor sent him to encourage the ruler of Angkor to provide tribute for the Mongol court and to initiate trade. It is no accident then that Zhou devoted some of his report to Angkor's products, which might appeal to the Mongols and to the Chinese. He wrote about ivory, four kinds of wine, rhinoceros horns, kingfisher feathers, cardamom, and other goods that the Chinese craved. At the same time, he found that the local population could serve as a market for Chinese silk, celadon ware, iron pots, combs, writing paper, and hemp. Judging from his report, trade could be mutually advantageous.

His report also betrays the condescension of the Chinese elite toward neighboring foreign peoples. He described these "southern barbarians" as coarse and ugly and emphasized the "shameful and wicked" effeminate among them and the so-called homeless savages. Although Zhou found many of the native practices objectionable, he had considerable interest in their exotic and particularly erotic customs, as this selection confirms.

Zhou's travels, together with the journeys of other voyagers, reveal the cosmopolitanism of the Mongol era. More Chinese envoys traveled to different states and learned more about the outside world than in earlier Chinese dynasties, attesting to the Mongols' promotion of Eurasian political and cultural interactions.

Young Girls

When a family is bringing up a daughter, her father and mother are sure to wish her well by saying, "May you have what really matters—in future may you marry thousands and thousands of husbands!"

When they are seven to nine years old—if they are girls from wealthy homes—or only when they are eleven—if they come from the poorest families—girls have to get a Buddhist monk or a Daoist to take away their virginity, in what is called *zhentan.*

So every year, in the fourth month of the Chinese calendar, the authorities select a day and announce it countrywide. The families whose daughters should be ready for *zhentan* let the authorities know in advance. The authorities first give them a huge candle. They make a mark on it, and arrange for it to be lit at dusk on the day in question. When the mark is reached the time for *zhentan* has come.

A month, fifteen days, or ten days beforehand, the parents have to choose a Buddhist monk or a Daoist. This depends on where the Buddhist and Daoist temples are. The temples often also have their own clients. Officials' families and wealthy homes all get the good, saintly Buddhist monks in advance, while the poor do not have the leisure to choose.

Wealthy and noble families give the monks wine, rice, silk and other cloth, betel nuts, silverware, and the like, goods weighing as much as a hundred piculs and worth two or three hundred ounces of Chinese silver. The smallest amount a family gives weighs ten to forty piculs, depending on how thrifty the family is.

The reason poor families only start dealing with the matter when their girls reach eleven is simply that it is hard for them to manage these things. Some wealthy families do also give money for poor girls' *zhentan*, which they call doing good work. Moreover in any one year a monk can only take charge of one girl, and once he has agreed to and accepted the benefits, he cannot make another commitment.

On the night in question a big banquet with drums and music is laid on for relatives and neighbors. A tall canopy is put up outside the entrance to the house, and various clay figurines of people and animals are laid out on top of it. There can be ten or more of these, or just three or four—or none at all in the case of poor families. They all have to do with events long ago, and they usually stay up for seven days before people start taking them down.

At dusk the monk is met with palanquin, parasol, drums, and music and brought back to the house. Two pavilions are put up, made of colorful silk. The girl sits inside one, and the monk inside the other. You can't understand what he's saying because the drums and music are making so much noise—on that night the night curfew is lifted. I have heard that when the time comes the monk goes into a room with the girl and takes away her virginity with his hand, which he then puts into some wine. Some say the parents, relatives and neighbors mark their foreheads with it, others say they all taste it. Some say the monk and the girl have sex together, others say they don't. They don't let Chinese see this, though, so I don't really know.

Toward dawn the monk is seen off again with palanquin, parasol, drums, and music. Afterward silk, cloth, and the like have to be given to the monk to redeem the body of the girl. If this is not done the girl will be the property of the monk for her whole life and won't be able to marry anyone else.

The instance of this that I saw took place early on the sixth night of the fourth month of the year *dingyou* in the Dade reign period (1297).

Before this happens, the parents always sleep together with their daughter; afterward, she is excluded from the room and goes wherever she wants without restraint or precaution. When it comes to marriage, there is a ceremony with the giving of gifts, but it is just a simple, easygoing affair. There are many who get married only after leading a dissolute life, something local custom regards as neither shameful nor odd.

On a *zhentan* night up to ten or more families from a single alley may be involved. On the city streets people are out meeting

Buddhist monks and Daoists, going this way and that, and the sounds of drums and music are everywhere.

Zhou Daguan, *A Record of Cambodia*, translated by Peter Harris (Seattle: University of Washington Press, 2007), 56–58.

DISCUSSION QUESTIONS

1. What does this section of Zhou's report reveal about Chinese attitudes toward foreigners?
2. Most travelers during the *Pax Mongolica* were merchants and missionaries, but Zhou was an official emissary. Why would the Mongol rulers of China send Zhou on this official embassy to the modern country of Cambodia?

E. A. Wallis Budge, The Monks of Kublai Khan, Emperor of China

Rabban Sauma (d. 1294) was the first man from China attested to have reached Europe. A Nestorian Christian, he and another monk received permission from the Mongols in China to make a pilgrimage to the Holy Land. They arrived in Mongol-ruled Iran to discover that the Mamluks, an Islamic dynasty, controlled the Holy Land, preventing the two Nestorian clerics from fulfilling their dream. The two decided to remain in the Middle East, leading to Rabban Sauma's great adventure.

In 1287, the Il-Khan Arghun sought to propose an alliance with the Europeans to topple the Mamluk dynasty, their common enemy. He recruited Rabban Sauma as his envoy, and the Nestorian monk traveled to the Byzantine empire, Naples, Rome, Paris, Bordeaux, and Genoa. He met with King Philip IV of France and King Edward I of England, both of whom professed interest in a crusade against the Mamluks, an extraordinary alliance had it been effected. However, both kings faced domestic insurrections and conflicts with other European states, preventing them from pursuing such an entente. Moreover, they may not have trusted the Mongols; after all, the Mongols had conquered much of Russia and attacked Hungary and Poland.

Rabban Sauma returned to the Il-Khanate, believing that he had achieved a diplomatic coup. He then produced an account of his travels, much of which deals with his theological discussions with the College of Cardinals and the Pope, the sacred sites and churches he visited, and the hazards of travel. This account offers a unique Eastern view of the West. His diplomatic mission turned out to be a failure but offered the opportunity for endless discussion and speculation about the consequences of such an alliance and the potential defeat of the most important remaining Islamic dynasty.

There are many Mongols who are Christians. For many of the sons of the Mongol kings and queens have been baptized and confess Christ. And they have established churches in their military camps, and they pay honour to the Christians, and there are among them many who are believers. Now the king [of the Mongols], who is joined in the bond of friendship with the Catholicus, hath the desire to take Palestine, and the countries of Syria, and he demandeth from you help in order to take Jerusalem. He hath chosen me and hath sent me to you because, being a Christian, my word will be believed by you."

* * *

Rabban Sawma in Fransa or Frangestan

Afterwards they went to the country of Pariz (Paris), to king Fransis [*i.e.* Philippe IV le Bel]. And the king sent out a large company of men to meet them, and they brought them into the city with great honour and ceremony. Now the territories of the French king were in extent more than a month's journey. And the king of France assigned to Rabban Sawma a place wherein to dwell, and three days later sent one of his Amirs to him and summoned him to his presence. And when he had come the king stood up before him and paid him honour, and said unto him, "Why hast thou come? And who sent thee?" And Rabban Sawma said unto him, "King Arghon and the Catholicus of the East have sent me concerning the matter of Jerusalem." And he showed him all the matters which he knew, and he gave him the letters which he had with him, and the gifts, that is to say, presents which he had brought. And the king of France answered him, saying, "If it be indeed so that the Mongols, though they are not Christians, are going to fight against the Arabs for the capture of Jerusalem, it is meet especially for us that we should fight [with them], and if our Lord willeth, go forth in full strength."

And Rabban Sawma said unto him, "Now that we have seen the glory of thy kingdom, and have looked upon the splendour of your strength with the eye of flesh, we ask you to command the men of the city to show us the churches, and the shrines, and the relics of the saints, and everything else which is found with you, and is not to be seen in any other country, so that when we return we may make known in the [various] countries what we have seen with you." Then the king commanded his Amirs, saying. "Go forth and show them all the wonderful things which we have here, and afterwards I myself will show [them] what I have." And the Amirs went out with them.

And Rabban Sawma and his companions remained for a month of days in this great city of Paris, and they saw everything that was in it. There were in it thirty thousand scholars [*i.e.* pupils] who were engaged in the study of ecclesiastical books of instruction, that is to say of commentaries and exegesis of all the Holy Scriptures, and also of profane learning; and they studied wisdom, that is to say philosophy, and [the art of] speaking (rhetoric?), and [the art of] healing, geometry, arithmetic, and the science of the planets and the stars; and they engaged constantly in writing [theses], and all these pupils received money for subsistence from the king. And they also saw one Great Church wherein were the funerary coffers of dead kings, and statues of them in gold and in silver were upon their tombs. And five hundred monks were engaged in performing commemoration services in the burial-place [*i.e.* mausoleum] of the kings, and they all ate and drank at the expense of the king. And they fasted and prayed continually in the burial-place of those kings. And the crowns of those kings, and their armour, and their apparel were laid upon their tombs. In short Rabban Sawma and his companions saw everything which was splendid and renowned.

* * *

Rabban Sawma goes to the King of England [*i.e.* Edward I]

And they went forth from that place, that is to say, from Paris, to go to the king of England, to Kasonia (Gascony?). And having arrived in twenty days at their city [Bordeaux?], the inhabitants of the city went forth to meet them, and they asked them, "Who are ye?" And Rabban Sawma and his companions replied, "We are ambassadors, and we have come from beyond the eastern seas, and we are envoys of the King, and of the Patriarch, and the Kings of the Mongols." And the people made haste and went to the king and informed him [of their arrival], and the king welcomed them gladly, and the people introduced them into his presence. And those who were with Rabban Sawma straightway gave to the king the Pukdana [*i.e.* letter of authorisation] of King Arghon, and the gifts which he had sent to him, and the Letter of Mar Catholicus. And [King Edward] rejoiced greatly, and he was especially glad when Rabban Sawma talked about the matter of Jerusalem. And he said, "We the kings of these cities bear upon our bodies the sign of the Cross, and we have no subject of thought except this matter. And my mind is relieved on the subject about which I have been thinking, when I hear that King Arghon thinketh as I think." And the king commanded Rabban Sawma to celebrate the Eucharist, and he performed the Glorious Mysteries; and the king and his officers of state stood up, and the king partook of the Sacrament, and made a great feast that day.

Then Rabban Sawma said unto the king, "We beseech thee, O king, to give [thy servants] the order to show us whatever churches and shrines there are in this country, so that when we go back to the Children of the East we may give them descriptions of them."

* * *

And that same night [the Arabs] seized Mar Catholicus in his Cell (*i.e.* palace) in Maraghah, and outside the building no man knew anything about the seizure of him until the day broke. And from the morning of that day, which was the second day of the week (Monday) they went into his Cell and plundered everything that was in it, both that which was old and that which was new, and they did not leave even a nail in the walls.

And on the night of the third day of the week (Tuesday) following, which was the 27th day of 'Ilul (September), the Catholicus was buffeted the whole night long by those who had seized him. And in respect of the venerable men who were with him, the Arabs tied some of them up naked with ropes; others cast aside their apparel and took to flight, and others cast themselves down from high places [and perished]. And they suspended the Catholicus by a rope head downwards, and they took a cloth used for cleaning, that is to say, a duster, and they put ashes in it, and tied it over his mouth, and one prodded him in the breast with a skewer (*bukshina*), saying, "Abandon this Faith of thine that thou perish not; become a Hagaraya (Muhammadan) and thou shalt be saved." And the Catholicus, weeping, answered them never a word. And they smote him with a stick on his thighs and seat (*i.e.* posterior). And they also took him up on to the roof of the Cell, saying, "Give us gold and we will let thee go; point out to us thy treasures, show us the things which thou hast hidden away, and reveal to us thy hiding-things and we will let thee go."

* * *

And then a great tumult took place, and the peoples of the Arabs came with a great rush to destroy the great church of Mar Shalita, the holy martyr, and they destroyed it. And they took everything that was in it, the veils (or hangings), and the vessels and other objects used in the service. And the uproar made by their outcries, and the storm of their shoutings shook almost the earth itself and the inhabitants thereof. Peradventure the reader of this history, since he was not caught in the middle of that storm, may think that the writer is telling a fabulous story; but to speak the real truth, he who stateth what is here written calleth God to witness, that it is impossible for even one of the events which took place to be adequately described and written!

* * *

King Kazan Pays Honour to Mar Yahbh-Allaha

Now when the sun had descended into the sign of the Ram, and creation was warmed a little, the Catholicus sent one of the monks of the Cell to the victorious King Kazan, to the place called Mughan, the winter station of all the Mongol Kings, to bless him and to inform [him] concerning the events that had happened to him. And when that monk arrived at the Camp, and he had taken care to see all the Amirs, they introduced him into the presence of the victorious king, and he declared unto him in their entirety all the words which Mar Catholicus had spoken to him saying, "Blessed is thy throne, O king, and it shall stand firm for ever, and thy seed shall be surely seated thereon for ever." And the king asked, "Why did not the Catholicus come to us?" and the monk replied, "Because of the confused state [of his mind]. He was hung up, and cruelly beaten, and his head touched the earth. Through the severe pain which hath been roused in him he was unable to come to do homage to the king, and it is for this reason that he hath sent me to pronounce his blessing upon thee, O my lord, the king. But when the victorious king shall arrive in peace at Tabhriz, whether the Catholicus be sick or whether he be well, he will come to salute thee and do homage to thee."

And God caused these words to find mercy in the eyes of the king, and he gave to the Catholicus a Pukdana, according to custom, in which it was laid down that poll-tax should not be exacted from the Christians; that none of them shall abandon his Faith; that the Catholicus shall live in the state to which he hath been accustomed; that he shall be treated with the respect due to his rank; that he shall rule over his Throne; and shall hold the staff of strength over his dominion [*i.e.* that he shall wield his sceptre with vigour and determination]. And he promulgated an Edict throughout all countries, and addressed it to all the Amirs by their names, and to the soldiers, ordering them to give back everything which they had taken from the Catholicus or from the holy old men by force, and to give back to him what those men of Baghdad and their envoys, whom we have mentioned above, had taken. Moreover, he allotted and despatched to the Catholicus five thousand *dinars* (£2,500) for his expenses, saying, "These will serve him as a supply until he cometh to us."

E. A. Wallis Budge, *The Monks of Kublai Khan, Emperor of China* (London: Religious Tract Society, 1928), 174, 182–86, 210–11, 213, 220–22.

DISCUSSION QUESTIONS

1. Why was Rabban Sauma an ideal choice as an envoy to the Pope and the European monarchs?
2. After his audiences with the kings of France and England, why did Rabban Sauma request visits to churches or to sacred sites?
3. Did the persecution of Nestorians and the Catholicus in the Il-Khanate fit in with general Mongol policy? What does such persecution reveal about the Il-Khanate?

Part VI
Collapse of the Mongol Empire

Juvaini, The History of the World Conqueror

The Persian historian Juvaini devoted most of his work to descriptions of the Mongols' military campaigns, especially those in Central Asia. However, he was also fascinated by the roles elite women played in Mongol society. In this selection, he documents their involvement in the first major conflict within the Mongol confederation.

See the headnote on p. 70 for additional information on this text.

Of Toregene Khatun

When the decree of God Almighty had been executed and the Monarch of the World, the Hatim of the Age, Qa'an, had passed away, Güyük, his eldest son, had not returned from the campaign against the Qifchaq, and therefore in accordance with precedent the dispatch of orders and the assembling of the people took place at the door of the *ordu* or palace of his wife, Möge Khatun, who, in accordance with the Mongol custom, had come to him from his father, Chingiz-Khan. But since Töregene Khatun was the mother of his eldest sons and was moreover shrewder and more sagacious than Möge Khatun, she sent messages to the princes, i.e. the brothers and nephews of Qa'an, and told them of what had happened and of the death of Qa'an, and said that until a Khan was appointed by agreement someone would have to be ruler and leader in order that the business of the state might not be neglected nor the affairs of the commonweal thrown into confusion; in order, too, that the army and the court might be kept under control and the interests of the people protected.

Chaghatai and the other princes sent representatives to say that Töregene Khatun was the mother of the princes who had a right to the Khanate; therefore, until a *quriltai* was held, it was she that should direct the affairs of the state, and the old ministers should remain in the service of the Court, so that the old and new *yasas* might not be changed from what was the law.

Now Töregene Khatun was a very shrewd and capable woman, and her position was greatly strengthened by this unity and concord. And when Möge Khatun shortly followed in the wake of Qa'an, by means of finesse and cunning she obtained control of all affairs of state and won over the hearts of her relatives by all kind of favours and kindnesses and by the sending of gifts and presents. And for the most part strangers and kindred, family and army inclined towards her, and submitted themselves obediently and gladly to her commands and prohibitions, and came under her sway. *The Prophet of God (may God bless him and give him peace!) hath said: 'Hearts were formed to love them that use them well and to hate them that use them ill.'* And all manner of men bent their steps towards her; while Chinqai and the other ministers of Qa'an continued to perform their duties as before, and the governors on every side remained at their posts.

* * *

Of Fatima Khatun

At the time of the capture of the place in which there lies the Holy Shrine of 'Ali ar-Riza *(upon whom be the most excellent of blessings and benedictions!)*, she was carried off into captivity. It so chanced that she came to Qara-Qorum, where she was a procuress in the market; and in the arts of shrewdness and cunning the wily Delilah could have been her pupil. During the reign of Qa'an she had constant access to the *ordu* of Töregene Khatun; and when times changed and Chinqai withdrew from the scene, she enjoyed even greater favour, and her influence became paramount; so that she became the sharer of intimate confidences and the depository of hidden secrets, and the ministers were debarred from executing business, and she was free to issue commands and prohibitions. And from every side the grandees sought her protection, especially the grandees of Khorasan. And there also came to her certain of the *sayyids* of the Holy Shrine, for she claimed to be of the race of the great *sayyids*.

When Güyük succeeded to the Khanate, a certain native of Samarqand, who was said to be an 'Alid, one Shira, the cupbearer of Qadaq, hinted that Fatima had bewitched Köten, which was why he was so indisposed. When Köten returned, the malady from which he was suffering grew worse, and he sent a messenger to his brother Güyük to say that he had been attacked by that illness because of Fatima's magic and that if anything happened to him Güyük should seek retribution from her. Following on this message there came tidings of Köten's death. Chinqai, who was now a person of authority, reminded Güyük of the message, and he sent an envoy to his mother to fetch Fatima. His mother refused to let her go saying that she would bring her herself. He sent again several times, and each time she refused him in a different way. As a result his relations with his mother became very bad, and he sent the man from Samarqand with instructions to bring Fatima by force if his mother should still delay in sending her or find some reason for refusing. It being no longer possible to excuse herself she agreed to send Fatima; and shortly afterwards she passed away. Fatima was brought face to face with Güyük, and was kept naked, and in bonds, and hungry and thirsty for many days and nights; she was plied with all manner of violence, severity, harshness and intimidation; and at last she confessed to the calumny of a slanderous talebearer and avowed her falseness. Her upper and lower orifices were sewn up, and she was rolled up in a sheet of felt and thrown into the river.

One thou raisest up and givest him a kingdom, and then
thou castest him into the sea to the fishes.

* * *

After Ulugh-Noyan's death Qa'an commanded that as long as he lived affairs of state should be administered in accordance with the counsel of his wife Sorqotani Beki, the niece of Ong-Khan, by whom he had his eldest sons, Mengü Qa'an, Qubilai, Hülegü and Arigh Böke, and that the above-mentioned sons, the army and the people, great and small, should be under the control of her command and prohibition, her loosening and binding, and should not turn their heads from her commandment. Now in the management and education of all her sons, in the administration of affairs of state, in the maintenance of dignity and prestige and in the execution of business, Beki, by the nicety of her judgement and discrimination, constructed such a basis and for the strengthening of these edifices laid such a foundation that no turban-wearer (*kulab-dar*) would have been capable of the like or could have dealt with these matters with the like brilliance. In any business which Qa'an undertook, whether with regard to the weal of the Empire or the disposal of the army, he used first to consult and confer with her and would suffer no change or alteration of whatever she recommended. The ambassadors and *elchis* too held her in great honour and respect; and the dependents and subjects of her Court in nearest and farthest East and West were distinguished from those of all the other princes by the dignity and protection they enjoyed, and because of her zealous concern for each of them individually their lives were contented and carefree. And the tax-gatherers, the *shahnas* and the army, for fear of her punishment and discipline, were fain to deal equitably with the people. And whenever there was a *quriltai* or assembly of the princes, and there was great elegance, and decoration, and adornment, and embellishment on the part of everybody, she was distinguished above them all with respect both to her retinue and to her troops. And her protection was such that when during the reign of Qa'an certain *maliks* were involved in a dispute with some of her dependents regarding the tax and *qupchur* to be levied on her subjects and had committed excesses, she sent messengers to have the *maliks* brought to her presence and after the establishment of evidence had them put to death.

As for her control and management of her sons, though each of them is a khan and a personality in the mould of his intellect, and superior to all [other] princes in shrewdness and sagacity, nevertheless, whenever by reason of the occurrence of a death they awaited the accession of a new khan, she would allow no change or alteration of the ancient ordinances or *yasas*, although, in fact, they had the licence of authority and of command and prohibition. So it was that when Güyük Khan was raised to the Khanate and there was search and inquiry as to which of the princes had deviated from the *yasa* and established custom and had issued *paizas* [passports] and *yarlighs,* he commanded that every order and *paiza* that had been issued since the death of Qa'an should be withdrawn. And in the *quriltai*, in the presence of all, most of the decrees which they had issued with regard to the assignment of taxes and the appointment and dismissal of tax-gatherers were laid before the princes [responsible for them]. All were put to shame save only Beki and her sons, who had not swerved a hair's breadth from the law, and this because of her great wisdom, self-discipline and consideration of the latter end of things, whereof even wise and experienced *men* are negligent.

And if women were like unto her, then would
women be superior to men.

And at the time of the accession of Mengü Qa'an to the throne of the Khanate the same thing happened again, because after Güyük Khan's death everyone had issued his own decrees.

As for Beki, from the time when Ulugh-Noyan passed away, she had won favour on all sides by the bestowing of gifts and presents upon her family and kindred and dispensing largesse to troops and strangers and so rendered all subject to her will and planted love and affection in everyone's heart and soul, so that when the death of Güyük Khan occurred most men were agreed and of one mind as to the entrusting of the keys of the Khanate to her son Mengü Qa'an. For the report of her wisdom and prudence and the fame of her counsel and sagacity had spread to all parts, and none would gainsay her word.

Furthermore, in the management of her household and in the ceremonial of her court she laid for kinsmen and stranger such a foundation as the khans of the world had not been capable of.

And so she continued until the time when God Almighty through the mediation of her experience laid the bride of kingship in the bosom of Mengü Qa'an's distinction. And her hand was ever open in munificence and benefaction, and although she was a follower and devotee of the religion of Jesus she would bestow alms and presents upon *imams* and *shaikhs* and strove also to revive the sacred observances of the faith of Mohammed (*may God bless him and give him peace!*). And the token and proof of this statement is that she gave 1000 silver *balish* that a college (*madrasa*) might be built in Bokhara, of which pious foundation the *shaikh-al-Islam* Saif-ad-Din of Bakharz should be administrator and superintendent; and she commanded that villages should be bought, an endowment made and teachers and students accommodated [in the college]. And always she would send alms to all parts to be distributed among the poor and needy of the Moslems; and so she continued until in Zul-Hijja of the year 649 [February–March, 1252], when the Destroyer of Delights sounded the note of departure.

The History of the World Conqueror, translated by John Boyle (Manchester: Manchester University Press, 2 vols., 1958), 239–41, 244–46, 550–53.

DISCUSSION QUESTIONS

1. Describe the different portraits of Toregene and Sorghaghtani Beki. Analyze their political maneuverings.
2. Judging from these selections, what is the role of women in Mongol society?
3. Can you generalize about the status of ordinary women from these selections?
4. Judging from the portrait of Fatima, what was the court's attitude toward Islam?

Rashid al-Din, Compendium of Chronicles

In this selection, Rashid al-Din shows the disunity and resulting conflicts among the Mongols, which weakened them and eventually led to the collapse of the Mongol Empire.

See the headnote on p. 59 for more information on this text.

The eldest of Ögetei Qa'an's wives, Töregene Khatun, governed [the realm], and during this period confusion found its way into the borders and center of the Empire. Qa'an had made his grandson Shiremün his heir-apparent, but Töregene Khatun and some of the emirs objected, saying that Güyük Khan was older, and they again summoned Batu to take part in the enthronement. Though he was offended with them and apprehensive because of the alarming nature of the past events, he set out, proceeding at a slow pace. Before his arrival and without the attendance of *aqa* and *ini* [princes], they arbitrarily settled the Khanate upon Güyük Khan. Güyük Khan was afflicted with a chronic disease, and on the pretext that the climate of his old *yurt*, which his father had given him, was beneficial to his condition, he set out with a large army for the region of Emil-Qochin. When he approached this area, Batu became a little apprehensive. Sorqoqtani Beki, the eldest wife of Tolui Khan, because of the foundation of friendship that had been laid and consolidated between Jochi Khan and Tolui Khan and the families of either side since the time of Chingiz-Khan, sent the message that Güyük Khan's coming to that region was not devoid of some treachery. On that account, his apprehension was increased and he awaited the arrival of Güyük Khan with vigilance and caution.

* * *

History of Tolui Khan's Wife, Sorqoqtani Beki, and his sons after his death until the time when they became *qa'ans* and rulers through the efforts and endeavors of their mother and as the result of her ability and intelligence

After the death of Tolui Khan his sons together with their mother were in attendance on Ögetei. He greatly honored and respected them and used to grant their petitions immediately. One day Sorqoqtani Beki asked Qa'an for one of the *ortaqs* [Trades]. He made difficulties about it, and Sorqoqtani Beki wept and said: "He that was my longing and desire, for whom did he sacrifice himself? For whose sake did he die?" When these words reached Qa'an's ear he said "Sorqoqtani Beki is right." And he begged her pardon and granted her request. She was extremely intelligent and able and towered above all the women in the world, possessing in the fullest measure the qualities of steadfastness, virtue, modesty, and chastity. Thanks to her ability, when her sons were left by their father, some of them still children, she went to great pains in their education, teaching them various accomplishments and good manners and never allowing the slightest sign of strife to appear amongst them. She caused their wives also to have love in their hearts for one another, and by her prudence and counsel [she] cherished and protected her sons, their children and grandchildren, and the great emirs and troops that had been left by Chingiz-Khan and Tolui Khan and were now attached to them. And perceiving her to be extremely intelligent and able, they never swerved a hair's breadth from her command. And just as, when Chingiz-Khan was left an orphan by his father, his mother, Hö'elün Eke, trained him and all the army, sometimes even going into battle herself and equipping and maintaining them until Chingiz-Khan became independent and absolute, and attained to the degree of world-sovereignty, and accomplished great things thanks to his mother's endeavors, so too Sorqoqtani Beki followed the same path in the training of her children. It is said, however, that in one respect she was more long-suffering than the mother of Chingiz-Khan and won the palm from her for constancy. After a time Chingiz-Khan gathered from a cryptic remark of his mother that she wanted a husband and he gave her in marriage to Menglik Echige. [In the same way] Ögetei Qa'an sent for Sorqoqtani Beki to give her in marriage to his son Güyük and sent———[1]as his ambassador in this affair. When he had delivered Qa'an's *yarligh*, she answered: "How is it possible to alter the terms of the *yarligh*? and yet my thought is only to bring up these children until they reach the stage of manhood and independence, and to try to make them well mannered and not liable to go apart and hate each other so that, perhaps, some great thing may come of their unity." Since she had no mind for Güyük Khan and had rejected that proposal by this excuse, no doubt was left that she did not wish to marry. On this account she was considered superior to Hö'elün Eke, the mother of Chingiz-Khan.

During the reign of Ögetei Qa'an, after Tolui Khan's death, two *hazaras* of Süldüs, part of the army belonging to Tolui Khan and his sons, were given by [Ögetei] to his son Köten on his own authority without consulting the *aqa* and *ini*. The *tümen* and *hazara*

[1] Blank in all the MSS.

commanders who had been connected with Yeke-Noyan, such as———,[2] when they learnt of this action, made a joint statement before Sorqoqtani Beki, Möngke Qa'an, and their *aqa* and *ini*, to this effect: "These two *hazaras* of Süldüs troops belong to us by virtue of the *yarligh* of Chingiz-Khan, and now he is giving them to Köten. How can we allow this and in so doing contravene the edict of Chingiz-Khan? We shall make representations to the Qa'an." Sorqoqtani Beki replied: "What you say is true, but we have no shortage of possessions, whether inherited or acquired, and are in no kind of need. The army and we ourselves all belong to the Qa'an: he knows what he is doing, and it is for him to command and for us to submit and obey." And when Sorqoqtani Beki spoke thus, the commanders were silenced, and all who heard approved.

There is no doubt that it was through her intelligence and ability that she raised the station of her sons above that of their cousins and caused them to attain to the rank of *qa'ans* and emperors. The main reason that her sons became *qa'ans* was as follows. When Ögetei Qa'an died, Töregene Khatun did not allow Shiremün, who by virtue of his will was heir-apparent, to become *qa'an*, but ruled for awhile herself. When she set up her eldest son Güyük Khan as Emperor, Batu, who was the senior of them all, did not attend on the excuse that he was suffering from gout. Güyük Khan was offended at this and in his heart was meditating an act of treachery against Batu. On the pretext that the climate of Emil was good for his sickness, he set out in that direction. Sorqoqtani Beki, learning of his intention, secretly sent a message and warned Batu. Shortly afterward Güyük died, and the sons and kinsmen of Ögetei Qa'an wished to set up Shiremün as Qa'an, but first they sent to summon Batu. He said: "I am suffering from gout. It would be better for them to come to me." Töregene Khatun and the family of Ögetei Qa'an objected to this suggestion saying: "Chingiz-Khan's capital is here: why should we go thither?" Now Batu was old and honored and the eldest of all the princes; and his was the right to nominate a new ruler. Sorqoqtani Beki said to her eldest son Möngke Qa'an: "The others will not go to Batu, and yet he is the senior of them all and is ill. It is for thee to hasten to him as though upon a visit to a sick bed." In

[2] Blank in all the MSS.

obedience to his mother's command he proceeded thither and Batu, in gratitude for this gesture and in consideration of previous obligations, swore allegiance to him and set him up as Qa'an.

***

History of How Mengeser Noyan Examined the case of the emirs who had plotted treason along with the princes

The next day he ordered the detention of the group of *noyans* and emirs, men such as Elchitei the great *noyan*, Taunal, Jangi, Qankhitai, Sorghan, Taunal the Younger, Toghan, and Yasa'ur, each of whom regarded himself as of such rank that the highest heaven had no power over him, and also a number of other *tümen* commanders and leaders, whom it would take too long to name. And he commanded the Emir Mengeser, the *yarghuchï*, to sit and hold an inquiry along with a number of other emirs. They began their questioning and continued the trial for several days. They put the questions in an extremely subtle manner, so that in the end the contradictions in their words became apparent, no doubt remained as to their conspiracy, and they all together confessed and admitted their guilt, saying: "We had made such a conspiracy and plotted treason." Möngke Qa'an, following his laudable custom, wished to accord them the honor of pardon and forgiveness, but the *noyans* and emirs said: "To neglect and delay removal of an enemy when the opportunity presents itself is remote from the highway of rectitude."

> Wherever thou oughtest to make a scar, when thou puttest a salve thereon, it availeth not.

Realizing that their words were spoken out of sincerity and not from motives of self-interest or hypocrisy, he ordered them all to be bound and imprisoned, and for awhile he reflected about their fate.

One day when he was seated in his Court on the throne of empire and sovereignty, he ordered each of the emirs and pillars of state to recite a *bilig* about the guilty men based upon what he had seen. Each of them said something within the limits of his understanding and to the extent of his knowledge, but none of this took root in his heart. Mahmud Yalavach was standing at the far end of the assembly. Said Möngke Qa'an: "Why does not this *ebügen* [old man] say something?" They said to Yalavach: "Come forward and speak." He replied: "In the presence of kings it is better to be an ear than a tongue. However I remember one story which I will relate if I am so commanded." "Speak," said Möngke Qa'an. Yalavach related as follows: "When Alexander had conquered most of the countries of the world he wished to go to India, but his emirs and chief men set foot outside the highway of obedience and loyalty and each of them breathed the breath of despotism and autocracy. Alexander was at a loss and sent a messenger to Rum to Aristotle, his peerless vizier, to tell him of the refractoriness and arrogance of his emirs and to ask what measures he should take to deal with them. Aristotle went into a garden with the messenger and ordered the trees with large roots to be dug out and small, frail saplings to be planted in their stead. He gave no reply to the messenger, and when the latter grew tired [of waiting] he returned to Alexander and said: 'He gave me no answer.' 'What didst thou see him do?' asked Alexander. 'He went into a garden,' said the messenger, 'and pulled out the large trees and planted small branches in their stead.' 'He gave his answer' said Alexander, 'but thou didst not understand.' And he destroyed the despotic emirs who had been all-powerful and set up their sons in their stead."

Möngke Qa'an was extremely pleased with this story and realized that these people must be done away with and others maintained in their place. He ordered the emirs that were imprisoned and those who had incited the princes to rebellion and cast them into the gulf of so great a crime to be put to the sword of public execution. There were seventy-seven persons, all of whom were put to death.

* * *

As for Oghul-Qaimish, Khwaja's mother, she sent back the messenger saying: "You princes promised and gave a written undertaking that the kingship would always remain in the family of Ögetei Qa'an and you would not rebel against his descendants. And now you have not kept your word." When this message was delivered Möngke Qa'an was exceedingly angry and wrote the following *yarlïgh*: "The wives of Jochi-Qasar, Otchigin, and Bilgütei Noyan, who were the brothers of Chingiz-Khan, attended the counsel for the *quriltai*, but Oghul-Qaimish did not. If the *qams* and Qadaq, Chinqai, and Bala, who were the emirs of the *ordo* of Güyük Khan, should call or proclaim any one ruler or *khatun* and that person becomes ruler or *khatun* because of their words, they shall see what they shall see." And at once he sent a messenger to seize and bring her with her hands stitched together in raw hide. When she arrived she was sent with Qadaqach, the mother of Shiremün, to the *ordo* of Sorqoqtani Beki. Mengeser Yarghuchi stripped her naked, dragged her into court, and began to question her. She said: "How can others see a body which has been seen by none but a king?" Her guilt having been ascertained she was wrapped in felt and flung into the river. Chinqai too arrived, and he was dealt with by Danishmand Hajib in Ramadan of the year 650 [November–December, 1252].

In Besh-Balïq the *ïdï-qut* who was the leader of the idolaters, arranged with certain people to rise up on a Friday, when the Muslims were gathered together in the Friday mosque, and kill them all inside the mosque. A slave amongst them, who was informed of their plan, confessed Islam and, turning informer against them, demonstrated their guilt of this crime. The *ïdï-qut* was brought to the *ordo* and put on trial; and when he had confessed his guilt orders were given that he should be taken to Besh-Balïq and put to death on a Friday after prayers in the presence of the whole population.

History of How Möngke Qa'an Dispatched emirs in every direction to deal with the remainder of the rebels and how he pardoned their crime

Since some of the rebels were still left [hidden] in corners and it would have been difficult and would have taken a long time to bring them to Court, he sent Bala Yarghuchï with a group of *nökers* to the armies of Yesü-Möngke to inquire about these people and put to death all that had taken part in the conspiracy. And he sent another emir to Khitai charged with the same task.

And when the thought of those wicked men had been dismissed from his august mind the fair character of the fortunate Emperor required him to regard it as his first duty to respect the claims of kinship and consanguinity. He ordered Shiremün to accompany

Qubilai Qa'an, Naqu, and Jaghan Noyan to Khitai. As for Khwaja, out of gratitude to his wife, who had spoken praiseworthy words, he exempted him from taking part in the campaign and fixed his *yurt* in the region of the Selenge, which is near Qara-Qorum.

It was from this time that discord first appeared amongst the Mongols. Chingiz-Khan used to urge his sons to concord and unity and say: "As long as you are in agreement with one another fortune and triumph will be your friends, and your opponents will never gain the victory." By reason of this quality it has been possible for Chingiz-Khan and his posterity to conquer the greater part of the world. It is said that one day at the time of his first rising to power he was giving advice to his sons, and by way of an example he drew an arrow from his quiver, gave it to them, and said: "Break it." It was broken with only a little effort. Then he gave them two, which were also easily broken. And he went on increasing the number up to ten, and even the athletes and *bahadurs* of the army were unable to break them. "So it is with you also," he said. "As long as you support one another none will gain the victory over you and you will enjoy kingship and empire for a long period of time." Had the sultans of Islam followed the same path, their dynasty would not have been extirpated.

* * *

As for Arïq Böke, when he had fattened his horses in the summer and autumn, he did not keep his word but broke his promise and again went to war against [Qubilai] Qa'an. When he came to Yesüngge, who was stationed on the frontier of the region, he sent a messenger to say that he was coming to surrender. Having thus rendered him careless he fell upon him, routed and scattered him and his army, and restored the *ordos* of Chaghatai Khan and Kölgen as well as his own. Meanwhile, Yesüngge crossed the desert and made his way to the Qa'an, to whom he reported that a rebel was approaching. The Qa'an sent a messenger to Taghachar and gathered *cherigs.* He himself, Taghachar, Hulaquir, the son of Elchitei, and Narin-Qadan, with the armies they commanded, were the first [to be ready]. Hulaqur, Nachin Küregen, Derekei Küregen of the Ikires people, Oradai, and Qadan, each with his own *tümen*, proceeded in the van and fought well. As for Yesüngge, because his troops had been dispersed, he did not take part in this battle. The Qa'an, with the aforementioned armies, encountered Arïq Böke on the edge of the desert. They joined battle in a place called Abjiya-Köteger, in front of a hill called Khucha-Boldaq and a *na'ur* called Shimultai. Arïq Böke's army was defeated, and many of the Oirat tribesmen were killed. And when Arïq Böke was defeated with his army and fled, the Qa'an said: "Do not pursue them, for they are ignorant children. They must realize what they have done and repent." Ten days later Asutai, the son of Möngke Qa'an, who led Arïq Böke's rearguard, came to [Arïq Böke] and heard that the army of Taghachar and the other armies of the Qa'an had turned back. Arïq Böke and Asutai consulted together again and gave battle after mid-day on the edge of the sand desert called Elet, by Shirgen-Na'ur and Shilügelig hill. The Qa'an's army defeated the right wing of Arïq Böke's army, but the left wing and center stood firm till nightfall and in the night caused the Qa'an to withdraw. Both princes now retired with their armies and went to their own *ordos*, while most of their troops perished because of the great distance and their being on foot. In the winter both encamped in their own quarters and passed the spring and summer there. As for Arïq Böke, having several times asked Alghu to help him with arms and provisions and having received no response, he equipped an army and set out against him. *And God knows best what is right.*

* * *

The Emir Ahmad held the vizierate with honor for nearly 25 years, and Gau Finjan was associated with him for 9 years more with his customary rancor and envy; and after another 9 years he made another attempt on his life. It happened as follows. A certain Khitayan laid claim to properties of holiness and chastity and had made himself known in the *ordos* for his asceticism and piety. One day he pretended to be ill and sent some of his disciples to the emirs to say: "I shall die and come to life again after 40 days." They went and said this, and some people were sent to investigate. He was lying in his house in the manner of the dead and his children were mourning and lamenting over him. They thought that he was really dead, but after 40 days he came out and put about the story that he had come to life again. The Khitayans rallied around him and his affairs prospered greatly. Gau Finjan and the people of Daidu now went to him and consulted him about getting rid of the Emir Ahmad. As he was extremely cautious and alert, always having guards with him and his sleeping-place not being known, they decided to send two thousand men to a valley known as Chamchiyal, 4 parasangs from Daidu, in order to hold it, whilst a thousand men should go and spread the rumor that Jim-Gim was coming, so that the Emir Ahmad might come out to meet him and they might kill him.

Gau Finjan seated himself in a palanquin, for it is a custom of the rulers of those parts sometimes to sit in a palanquin and they often travel this way by night. And from that valley relays of heralds and messengers were dispatched to announce that Jim-Gim was coming. Ahmad was afraid of him. And all the men he sent in advance they killed. In the night they entered [the town] with torches and candles as is the custom of their rulers. When they drew near to the *qarshi*, the Emir Ahmad came out to take a cup, and they seized him and put him to death. As for the Emir Tergen, who was his *nöker*, he had acted with caution and had guessed that something was wrong. Standing at a distance with his *nökers* he took an arrow and shot Gau Finjan dead in the palanquin. The Khitayans fled and Tergen occupied the *qarshi*. There was a great deal of slaughter and tumult in the night, and the Khitayans went out [and hid themselves] in corners.

When this was reported to the Qa'an, he dispatched the Emir Bolad Aqa and Hantum Noyan at the head of an army to execute all of the Khitayans who had caused this disturbance. And he ordered 4,000 *balish* to be paid for the Emir Ahmad's funeral expenses and sent the great men and emirs to bury him with full honors.

Forty days later, the Qa'an sent for a large stone to set in his crown. It could not be found. Two merchants, who were there, came and said: "Previously we had brought a large stone for the Qa'an and [had] given it to the Emir Ahmad." The Qa'an said: "He did not bring it to me." And he sent to have it fetched from his house. It was found on his wife Injü Khatun and brought to the Qa'an. He was extremely annoyed and asked the merchants what should be the punishment of a slave who committed such a crime. They replied: "If alive he should be put to death, and if dead he should be taken out of his grave and publicly exposed as a warning to others." And the Khitayans for their part said to Jim-Gim: "He was thy enemy, and it was for that reason that we killed him." For that reason they had planted enmity toward him in the Qa'an's heart. Therefore, he ordered his body to be taken out of the grave and hanged in the market place by a rope tied to the feet, whilst wagons were driven over his head. Injü, his wife, was also put to death, and the forty other wives and four hundred concubines that he had were given away, whilst his possessions and effects were expropriated for the treasury. As for his sons, the Emir Ḥasan and the Emir Ḥusain, they were beaten until the skin came off, while his other children were given away. After [Aḥmad's] death, the vizierate was conferred upon an Uighur called Senge. * * *

The Successors of Genghis Khan, translated by John Boyle (New York: Columbia University Press, 1971), 120, 168–70, 211–12, 215–16, 256–57, 291–93.

DISCUSSION QUESTIONS

1. What did the conflict of Batu and Güyük reveal about problems for the Mongols? How would this struggle presage fragmentation of the Mongol Empire?
2. Why was the author so impressed with Sorghaghtani Beki? What role did she play in changes of Mongol attitudes toward governance?
3. What does Mahmud Yalavach's story disclose about the Muslim elite's knowledge of the world?
4. What were the larger implications of Möngke's purge? Whom was he purging?
5. Why would the author portray Arigh Böke in such a negative light?
6. One Mongol tradition was that the youngest son, in this case Arigh Böke, should be the successor. With Khubilai's defeat of Arigh Böke, how would many Mongols view Khubilai? How could this shape Khubilai's reign?

FOR FURTHER READING

Over the past three decades, increased interest in global history, as well as the excitement associated with the names "Chinggis Khan" and "Mongols," have spurred the writing of popular and scholarly books on the Mongol empire. Numerous articles have also appeared, but I will mention only books in this guide to further reading on the Mongols because journal essays are not readily accessible. Availability has been, for me, an important consideration in the compilation of this guide. Readability is another factor. I have chosen books that nonspecialist readers or college students can read comfortably and productively, and I have omitted works that are highly philological or are studded with lengthy notes of use to scholars but not highly illuminating for the general reader. I have kept the nonspecialist reader in mind in making these suggestions and thus include some reliable popularizations.

General Works

An excellent map of the Mongol empire at its height may be found in the December 1996 issue of *National Geographic*.

Atwood, Christopher. *Encyclopedia of Mongolia and the Mongol Empire*. New York: Facts on File, 2004. A general survey of the Mongol empire, with an accurate listing of names and dates.

Barfield, Thomas. *The Perilous Frontier*. Oxford: Blackwell Publishers, 1989. An anthropological analysis and interpretation of the role of the Mongols and other pastoral nomads in East Asian history.

Buell, Paul. *Historical Dictionary of the Mongol World Empire.* Lanham, MD: Scarecrow Press, 2003. A general survey of the Mongol empire, with an accurate listing of names and dates.

Chambers, James. *The Devil's Horsemen.* New York: Atheneum, 1979. A useful popularization of the Mongol invasions.

Fitzhugh, William, Morris Rossabi, and William Honeychurch, eds. *Genghis Khan and the Mongol Empire.* Seattle: University of Washington Press, 2009. The latest introduction to the history of the Mongols; includes an up-to-date accounting of current archeological excavations and is lavishly illustrated.

Jagchid, Sechin, and Paul Hyer. *Mongolia's Culture and Society.* Boulder, CO: Westview Press, 1979. A solid survey of Mongol customs, beliefs, and life cycles.

Lattimore, Owen. *Inner Asian Frontiers of China.* New York: American Geographical Society, 1940. Perhaps the most influential work on the peoples living north and west of China.

Morgan, David. *The Mongols.* Oxford: Basil Blackwell, 1986. This introductory history of the Mongol empire provides especially good coverage of the Il-Khanate in West Asia. A new edition was published in 2007 with a new preface.

Saunders, J. J. *The History of the Mongol Conquests.* London: Routledge and Kegan Paul, 1971. A useful popularization of the Mongol invasions.

Chinggis Khan and the Early Khans

The Secret History of the Mongols. Translated by Francis Cleaves. Cambridge, MA: Harvard University Press, 1982. An English translation of the only indigenous primary source on the Mongol era with a plethora of footnotes and technical data.

The Secret History of the Mongols. A Mongolian Epic Chronicle of the Thirteenth Century. Translated by Igor de Rachewiltz. Leiden: E. J. Brill, 2003. An English translation of the text with abundant footnotes and technical data.

Secret History of the Mongols. Translated by Paul Kahn. San Francisco: North Point Press, 1984. Offers a more accessible, poetic translation, based on Cleaves's work but with none of the scholarly paraphernalia.

Biran, Michal. *Chinggis Khan.* Oxford: Oneworld, 2007. Offers a sketch of Chinggis's life and career.

Changchun. *The Travels of an Alchemist.* Translated by Arthur Waley. London: Routledge and Kegan Paul, 1931. Arthur Waley, probably the most renowned translator of East Asian literature, translated an account of the Daoist traveler Changchun, who accompanied Chinggis during his campaigns in Central Asia.

Dunnell, Ruth. *Chinggis Khan.* New York: Prentice Hall, 2009. Another sketch of Chinggis's life and career.

Inoue, Yasushi. *Blue Wolf: A Novel on the Life of Chinggis Khan.* Translated by Joshua Fogel. New York: Columbia University Press, 2008. A fine novel about the Mongol leader, based on careful study.

Juvaini. *The History of the World Conqueror.* Translated by John Boyle. Manchester: Manchester University Press, 2 vols., 1958. An excellent translation of the work of Persian historian Juvaini, who is a primary source on Chinggis and his early successors.

Rashid al-Din. *The Successors of Genghis Khan.* Translated by John Boyle. New York: Columbia University Press, 1971. A partial translation of Rashid al-Din, who is also a primary source on Chinggis and his early successors.

Rashid al-Din. *Rashiduddin Fazlullah's Jami'u't Tawarikh: Compendium of Chronicles.* Translated by Wheeler Thackston. Cambridge, MA: Harvard University Department of Near Eastern Languages and Civilizations, 3 vols., 1998. A complete translation of Rashid al-Din.

Ratchnevsky, Paul. *Genghis Khan, His Life and Legacy.* Translated by Thomas Nivison Haining. Oxford: Blackwell, 2nd ed., 2006. The best biography on Chinggis Khan. The 2006 edition includes a new introduction by Morris Rossabi.

Vladimirtsov, B. I. *Life of Chingis Khan.* Translated by D. S. Mirsky. New York: Benjamin Blom, 1969 rpt. A Soviet interpretation of the life and career of the most prominent figure in Mongol history.

China under Mongol Rule

Chinese Art under the Mongols: The Yuan Dynasty (1279–1368). Cleveland: Cleveland Museum of Art, 1968. From the 1968 Cleveland Museum of Art exhibition of Yuan dynasty art, which Sherman Lee and Wai-kam Ho mounted.

Cahill, James. *Hills Beyond a River: Chinese Painting of the Yuan Dynasty.* New York: John Weatherhill, 1976. Discusses Zhao Mengfu and the other great Yuan painters.

Ch'en, Paul Heng-chao. *Chinese Legal Tradition under the Mongols.* Princeton, NJ: Princeton University Press, 1979. Discusses the Yuan dynasty legal code.

Conlan, Thomas. *In Little Need of Divine Intervention: Takezaki Suenaga's Scrolls of the Mongol Invasions.* Ithaca, NY: East Asia Program, Cornell University, 2001. Using contemporaneous Japanese scrolls, Conlan gleans new insights and information about Khubilai Khan's abortive invasion of Japan.

Dawson, Christopher, ed. *Mission to Asia.* New York: Harper & Row, 1966. Translations of the accounts of Christian missionaries to the Mongols.

de Rachewiltz, Igor. *Papal Envoys to the Great Khans.* London: Faber & Faber, 1971. Places the arrival of Christian missionaries in historical context.

De Bary, William Theodore, and Chan Hoklam, eds. *Yuan Thought: Chinese Thought and Religion under the Mongols.* New York: Columbia University Press, 1982. A collection of essays on Chinese religious and philosophical developments under the Mongols.

Delgado, James. *Khubilai Khan's Lost Fleet: In Search of a Legendary Armada.* Berkeley: University of California Press, 2008. Although Delgado is somewhat shaky on the history and significance of the attacks on Japan, he provides a survey of the important underwater excavations of the past twenty years, which have discovered weapons, seals, pottery, and even remains of one of the ships sunk during the 1281 typhoon.

Dunn, Ross. *The Adventures of Ibn Battuta.* Berkeley: University of California Press, 1986. Describes the travels of the Arab jurist Ibn Battuta in Asia and Africa.

Endicott-West, Elizabeth. *Mongolian Rule in China: Local Administration in the Yuan Dynasty.* Cambridge, MA: Harvard University Press, 1989. Deals with the government the Mongols imposed upon China during Khubilai's reign.

Franke, Herbert, and Denis Twitchett, eds. *The Cambridge History of China, Volume 6, Alien Regimes and Border States, 907–1368.* Cambridge: Cambridge University Press, 1994. The standard source for study of the various foreign dynasties that governed China from the tenth to the fourteenth centuries.

Gernet, Jacques. *Daily Life in China on the Eve of the Mongol Invasion, 1250–1276.* Translated by H. M. Wright. New York: Macmillan, 1962. A delightful social history of Southern Song China at its height, emphasizing family life, entertainments, food, and clothing. Khubilai Khan's troops overwhelmed the Southern Song in 1279.

Hsiao Ch'i-ch'ing. *The Military Establishment of the Yuan Dynasty.* Cambridge, MA: Harvard University Press, 1978. Concentrates on the military during Khubilai's reign.

Jay, Jennifer. *A Change in Dynasties.* Bellingham: Western Washington University, 1991. Portraits of Southern Song Chinese loyalists who resisted the Mongols even after they had established control over China and set up a dynasty.

Komaroff, Linda, and Stefano Carboni, eds. *The Legacy of Genghis Khan: Courtly Arts and Culture in Western Asia, 1256–1353.* New York: Metropolitan Museum of Art, 2002. A major exhibition of Yuan and Il-Khanate art, organized by Komaroff and Carboni at the Metropolitan Museum of Art and the Los Angeles County Museum of Art, produced this catalog, a richly illustrated study of the artistic, political, and economic interchanges between Yuan China and the Il-Khanate in West Asia.

Langlois, John, ed. *China under Mongol Rule.* Princeton, NJ: Princeton University Press, 1981. In the late 1970s, Langlois gathered specialists at a conference to discuss the important roles of Tibetans and Muslims at the Yuan Court, developments in art, and various other subjects. Langlois edited the resulting essays and gathered them in this collection.

Medley, Margaret. *Yuan Porcelain and Stoneware.* New York: Pitman Publishing, 1974. Examines Yuan dynasty ceramics, including the development of blue-and-white porcelains.

Petech, Luciano. *Central Tibet and the Mongols.* Rome: Instituto Italiano per il Medio ed Estremo Oriente, 1990. Delineates the earliest Tibeto-Mongol relations during the Yuan dynasty, which laid the foundations for the sixteenth- and seventeenth-century Mongol conversion to Tibetan Buddhism.

Rossabi, Morris. *Khubilai Khan: His Life and Times.* Berkeley: University of California Press, 1988. A biography of Khubilai Khan.

Rossabi, Morris. *Voyager to Xanadu.* New York: Kodansha, 1992; paperback: Berkeley: University of California Press, 2010. About the Nestorian Christian Rabban Sauma, the reverse Marco Polo, the first attested individual from China to reach Europe.

Schurmann, Herbert Franz. *Economic Structure of the Yuan Dynasty.* Cambridge, MA: Harvard University Press, 1956. Describes the Yuan dynasty's economy.

Smith, Paul, and Denis Twitchett, eds. *The Cambridge History of China, Volume 5, Part 1, The Sung Dynasty and Its Precursors, 907–1279.* Cambridge: Cambridge University Press, 2009. A political, economic, and military history of this glorious dynasty.

Smith, Paul, and Richard von Glahn, eds. *The Song-Yuan-Ming Transition in Chinese History.* Cambridge, MA: Harvard University Press, 2003. In the late 1990s, Smith and von Glahn, like Langlois, gathered specialists at a conference to discuss the position of women, developments in printing and medicine, and other subjects. Smith and von Glahn also edited the resulting essays and gathered them in this collection.

Watt, James, et al. *The World of Khubilai Khan.* New York: Metropolitan Museum of Art, 2010. The latest exhibit of Yuan dynasty art.

Zhou Daguan. *Record of Cambodia: The Land and Its People.* Translated by Peter Harris. Seattle: University of Washington Press, 2007. In the 1290s, the Yuan court dispatched an emissary named Zhou Daguan to Cambodia. Harris has translated Zhou's report on his travels, including a description of Angkor Wat.

Il-Khanate West Asia, the Golden Horde, and the West

Juvaini and Rashid al-Din, two Persian historians cited above, offer contemporaneous insight into the Mongol invasions and rule in West Asia. In addition, the catalog edited by Komaroff and Carboni is a guide to developments in Iranian art during the Il-Khanate.

Amitai-Preiss, Reuven. *Mongols and Mamluks: The Mamluk-Ilkhanid War, 1260–1281.* Cambridge: Cambridge University Press, 1995. Specialized studies on military engagements and ideology in West Asia.

Boyle, John, ed. *The Cambridge History of Iran: Volume 5: The Saljuq and Mongol Periods.* Cambridge: Cambridge University Press, 1968. Written forty years ago, still the standard English-language work on Mongol rule in West Asia.

Broadbridge, Ann. *Kinship and Ideology in the Islamic and Mongol Worlds.* Cambridge: Cambridge University Press, 2008. Specialized studies on military engagements and ideology in West Asia.

Calvino, Italo. *Invisible Cities.* Translated by William Weaver. New York: Harcourt Brace Jovanovich, 1974. The great Italian writer's fascinating novel is written in the form of dialogues between Marco Polo and Khubilai Khan.

Halperin, Charles. *Russia and the Mongol Impact on Medieval Russian History: Golden Horde.* Bloomington: Indiana University Press, 1985. Shows the Mongols' military, commercial, and political influences on Russia.

Jackson, Peter. *Mission of Friar William of Rubruck.* London: Hakluyt, 1990. Jackson provides a translation of the report of a Western emissary.

Jackson, Peter. *Mongols and the West, 1221–1410.* Harlow: Pearson Longman, 2005. The standard work on the subject, highly readable.

Lane, George. *Early Mongol Rule in Thirteenth-Century Iran: A Persian Renaissance.* New York: Routledge, 2003. A reliable popular account of Il-Khanate rule.

Morgan, David. *Medieval Persia, 1040–1797.* London: Longman, 1988. A synthetic and brief survey of Iran during the Mongol period.

Moule, A. C., and Paul Pelliot. *Marco Polo: The Description of the World.* London: George Routledge & Sons, 2 vols., 1938. The best translation of Marco's text, but not readily available. However, there are other acceptable translations, including ones by H. Yule and R. Latham.

Olschki, Leonardo. *Marco Polo's Asia.* Berkeley: University of California Press, 1960. A splendid and charming work stimulated by Marco's account.

Ostrowski, Donald. *Muscovy and the Mongols.* Cambridge: Cambridge University Press, 1998. Ostrowski tries to prove that the Mongols had considerable influence on Russia and to deflate arguments about their negative impact on Russia.

Vernadsky, George. *The Mongols and Russia.* New Haven, CT: Yale University Press, 1953. Like the Il-Khanate, the Golden Horde was, until recent times, depicted as an almost entirely negative influence on Russia. Vernadsky was among the first historians to portray the Mongols' influence in an unbiased way.

Wood, Frances. *Did Marco Polo Go to China?* London: Secker & Warburg, 1995. Wood presents a decidedly minority argument that Marco never reached China.

CREDITS

Rashid Al-Din: Excerpts from *The Successors of Genghis Khan*, trans. John Andrew Boyle, pp. 62–65, 77, 79–83, 120, 168–70, 211–12, 215–16, 256–57, 291–93. Copyright © 1971 Columbia University Press. Reprinted by permission of Columbia University Press.

Ibn Battuta: From *The Travels of Ibn Battuta, A.D. 1325–1354,* Vol. II, edited and translated by H. A. R. Gibb (Cambridge: Hakluyt Society, 1962), pp. 551–53. Reprinted by permission of the Hakluyt Society.

Baybars I of Egypt: "English Text of the Sirat," *Baybars I of Egypt*, edited by Dr. Syedah Fatimah Sadeque, M.A., Ph.D. (Pakistan: Oxford University Press, 1956), pp. 93–94, 156–57, 187–89. Reprinted by permission of Oxford University Press, Inc.

John Boyle: "Kirakos of Ganjak on the Mongols," translated by John Boyle, *Central Asiatic Journal* 8 (1963), pp. 201–4, 207. Reprinted by permission of the publisher, Harrassowitz Verlag.

E. A. Budge (trans.): "The Monks of Kublai Khan, Emperor of China" (London: The Religious Tract Society, 1928), pp. 174, 182–84, 185–86, 210–11, 213, 220–22. Reprinted by permission of the Lutterworth Press.

Li Chih Ch'ang: From *The Travels of an Alchemist*, translated by Arthur Waley, pp. 100–101, 114–18. Copyright © 1931 Routledge. Reproduced by permission of Taylor & Francis Books UK.

Zhou Daguan: "Young Girls," *A Record of Cambodia: The Land and Its People*, trans. Peter Harris, pp. 56–58. © 2007 by Peter Harris. Reprinted by permission of Silkworm Books.

Christopher Henry Dawson (trans.): "History of the Mongols," *Mission to Asia*, pp. 7–8, 16–17, 33–34, 36, 46–49. © Medieval Academy of America 1980. Reproduced by kind permission of Continuum International Publishing Group.

Igor de Rachewiltz: "The Letter of the Great Khan Güyüg to Pope Innocent IV (1246)," translated by J. A. Boyle for *Papal Envoys to the Great Khans*, by Igor de Rachewiltz (London: Faber & Faber Ltd), pp. 213–14. © Igor de Rachewiltz, 1971. We have made diligent efforts to contact the copyright holder to obtain permission to reprint this selection. If you have information that would help us, please write to Permissions Department, W. W. Norton & Company, Inc., 500 Fifth Avenue, New York NY 10110.

R. Fazlullah: Excerpts from "Jami'ut 'u't tawarikh: Compendium of Chronicles," trans. W. M. Thackston, eds. S. and G. Tekin, *Sources of Oriental Languages and Literatures.* Reprinted by permission of the Ottoman Studies Foundation.

Grigor of Akanc: Excerpts from "History of the Nation of Archers," translated by Robert Blake and Richard N. Frye, *Harvard Journal of Asiatic Studies* 12.3–4 (1949) 295, 297, 333, 335, 341, 343, 345. Reprinted by permission.

Prince Jin-Gim: From *Prince Jin-Gim's Textbook of Tibetan Buddhism*, translated and annotated by Constance Hoog, pp. 42–46. Copyright 1983 by E. J. Brill, Leiden, The Netherlands. We have made diligent efforts to contact the copyright holder to obtain permission to reprint this selection. If you have information that would help us, please write to Permissions Department, W. W. Norton & Company, Inc., 500 Fifth Avenue, New York NY 10110.

Ata Malik Juvaini: From *The History of the World-Conqueror,* pp. 41, 79–81, 97–100, 103–7, 117–22, 239–41, 244–46, 550–53, Collection of Representatives Works: Persian Series, 1958. © UNESCO 1958. Used by permission of UNESCO.

Paul Kahn: Excerpts from *The Secret History of the Mongols: The Origin of Chingis Khan* (North Point Press, 1984), based on F. W. Cleaves's translation, pp. 15–22, 44, 46, 92–93, 120–24, 166–67, 182. Copy-

INDEX